seasonal
plant
dyes

**Create your own beautiful botanical dyes,
plus four seasonal projects to make**

ALICIA HALL

Photographs by Alicia Hall

WHITE OWL

*For W, who adds the word 'maximus' to the end of
every flower to pretend he knows its Latin name. And to
Sebastianus Oleanderus, my favourite little plant*

First published in Great Britain in 2019 by
PEN & SWORD WHITE OWL
An imprint of Pen & Sword Books Ltd
Yorkshire – Philadelphia

Copyright © Alicia Hall, 2019
www.botanicalthreads.co.uk @botanical_threads

ISBN 9781526747235

Group Publisher: Jonathan Wright
Series Editor and Publishing Consultant: Katherine Raderecht
Art Director: Jane Toft
Production Editor: Elizabeth Raderecht

Printed and bound in India, by Replika Press Pvt. Ltd.

Pen & Sword Books Ltd incorporates the Imprints of Pen & Sword Books
Archaeology, Atlas, Aviation, Battleground, Discovery, Family History, History,
Maritime, Military, Naval, Politics, Railways, Select, Transport, True Crime,
Fiction, Frontline Books, Leo Cooper, Praetorian Press, Seaforth Publishing,
Wharncliffe and White Owl.

For a complete list of Pen & Sword titles please contact:

PEN & SWORD BOOKS LIMITED
47 Church Street, Barnsley, South Yorkshire S70 2AS, England
E-mail: enquiries@pen-and-sword.co.uk
Website: www.pen-and-sword.co.uk
or
PEN AND SWORD BOOKS
1950 Lawrence Rd, Havertown, PA 19083, USA
E-mail: Uspen-and-sword@casematepublishers.com
Website: www.penandswordbooks.com

contents

introduction

I discovered botanical dyeing during my time spent as a gardener for the National Trust, surrounded by a huge variety of beautiful trees, plants and vegetables. At the time, I stumbled across a horticulture book that mentioned dyeing with plants – a concept that was fascinating and entirely new to me. Inspired by what I read, I began gathering plants during my daily produce harvests in the National Trust kitchen garden, and my first foray into natural dyeing was an attempt to extract colour from carrot tops. After soaking the greenery in water overnight, I left a small cotton bag to sit in the magical green water, not quite believing that it would take the colour. To my amazement, I managed to dye the bag a beautiful chartreuse green. I was instantly hooked, and began months of intensive research and experimentation in order to deepen my understanding of the art of botanical dyeing, unlocking a whole new world of beautiful natural colour.

I'm passionate about introducing others to the magic of plant dyeing, and this book is designed to guide you through the dyeing seasons, teaching you the foundations of dyeing, showing you how to achieve the best results possible, and helping you build up your confidence and creativity. Sustainable methods of harvesting (both from the wild and from your own garden) are used throughout, to ensure that you get plenty of harvests from your plants – now and in the future.

Before we begin plant dyeing, it's important to know a little about fabrics and yarns. I've dedicated a chapter to how different fabrics and wools are made, what affect this has on the way plant dyes react with them, and the best way to dye and care for each one, as well as providing information on how they're sourced and manufactured.

One of the wonderful things about plant dyeing is that you can easily start learning this traditional craft without having to buy a huge amount of specialist equipment, and you'll find a list of simple tools – and what they're used for – in this book.

I've also included chapters on mordants (used to help plant dyes stick to fabric and wools) and modifiers (used to alter or enhance the colour of dye). Soya milk is perhaps the most surprising ingredient that I use as a mordant while plant dyeing, which is why I've dedicated a chapter to exploring why it works, as well as step-by-step instructions on how to use it. Modifiers such as aluminium and chrome can be toxic to both the dyer and the environment, so I've included alternatives which pose little or no risk.

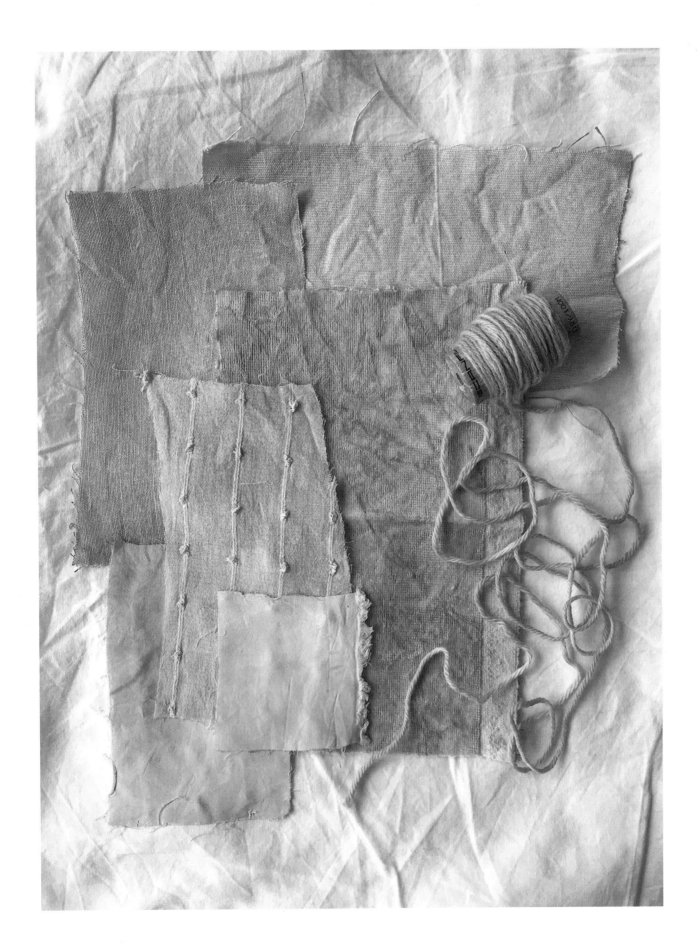

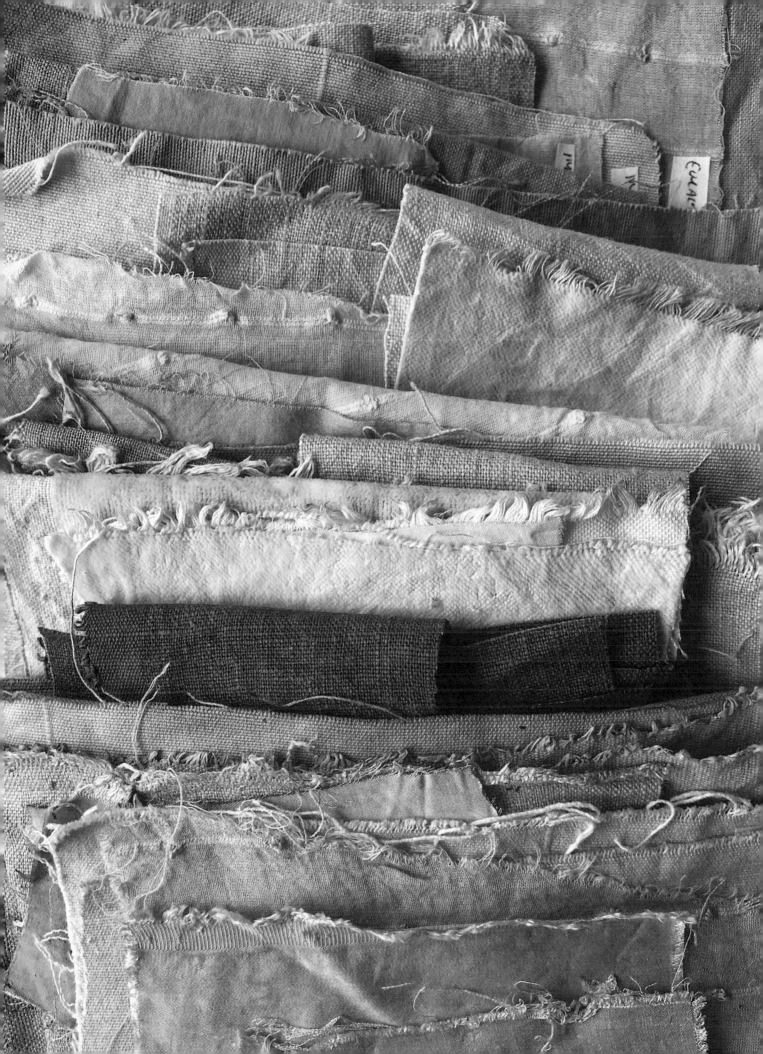

In the second part of this book, you'll start to get really creative as you learn how to extract colours from dye plants. Dyeing according to the seasons means that you'll be harvesting thoughtfully, helping the plants remain healthy, producing the best colours possible and ensuring more flowers for the following years. Cutting off flowers to harvest in the summer months will encourage new blooms; and cutting back some shrubs after flowering can improve plant health and promote healthy growth. Dividing some perennials in late winter or early spring will allow you to harvest the roots for dyeing, as well as reinvigorate the plant. And, of course, another advantage to dyeing seasonally is that you'll be harvesting plants when they're at their most abundant, which makes finding them in the wild much easier!

Plant dyeing is a craft that can be fitted into day-to-day life. It's often something that only requires a few minutes of dedication each day (popping out to the garden to harvest flowers, putting flowers or leaves in pots of water to soak, hanging fabrics out to dry, and so on) and can be incorporated easily into busy family or working life. Plants can be harvested from your own garden or foraged during weekend walks in the countryside. No dedicated space is needed, and fabrics can be left for days – or sometimes weeks – at a time in their dye pots, requiring just an occasional stir.

So why choose to use plant dyes over synthetic ones? Commercially, synthetic dyes are produced in large batches and have little or no variation in the colour between these batches, which means unlimited amounts of fabric can be dyed easily in order to mass-produce identical textile items. Synthetic dyes are available in a wide range of colours and the majority of them offer good colour-fastness when they're washed. Although clothes made from synthetic dyes haven't been found to pose any risk to the wearer, the dyes used to colour them are made up of chemical compounds that can be harmful to the people involved in their production. Lead and mercury are just two of the chemicals that are found in synthetic dyes, and these can be toxic to humans.

One of the main benefits of using plant dyes over synthetic dyes is that most natural dyes are harmless to the dyer and the waste products aren't harmful to the environment. Plants can be sent to the compost heap after the colour has been extracted from them, and used dye can be poured directly into the garden or down a drain without worrying about any negative impact to the surrounding area.

At this point, it's worth mentioning that there can be risks involved when working with poisonous plants to create dyes. Although these plants are usually only toxic when ingested or when they come into direct contact with skin, they should be used with caution and only in a well-ventilated area (ideally outside), and adequate protective clothing, such as gloves and a face mask, should be worn. A mask should also be worn when working with powdered plant extracts and mordants to avoid inhaling the fine particles, and, as a general safety measure, the dyeing area should be well ventilated because even harmless plants can become toxic when heated in concentrated quantities.

Whereas the production of synthetic dyes is seen as a science, the skill of plant dyeing is valued as an art form. Plant dyes are produced in smaller batches, most commonly by individual artisans and craftspeople wishing to keep this traditional skill alive.

Plant-dyed fabrics have a wonderful way of coordinating with each other, as they produce a gorgeous depth of colour that simply can't be mimicked using synthetic dyes. Colours from nature can produce varied results from different batches, so it's important to embrace plant dyeing's unpredictability! In my experience, the following factors can change the colour that a plant produces: the season that the plant was harvested; the soil that the plant was grown in; the temperature and pH of the water used to extract the dye and dye the fabric; the type of water used (filtered, tap or rain); the type of metal that the dye pot is made from; the residue left from plants previously used in the dye pot; the temperature of the water; the ratio of dye plant to fabric; the time that the dye plants are left soaking; the time that fabric is left soaking in the dye; and the variety of the plant used to make the dye.

Quite often, plant dyes have a reputation for fading quickly, not washing well and requiring subsequent dyeing to maintain the colours. Although there are a few plant colours that will always fade, I've found when using the correct dyeing technique and caring for fabrics properly, plant colours can last well and stand up to regular use.

Dyeing with plants is truly a craft that forces you to slow down and enjoy the process. This book encourages you to complete projects over long periods of time, spending weeks collecting and storing plants, creating the dye colour, and experimenting with different fabrics. At the end of each season chapter there's a beautiful modern sewing project that uses fabrics that have been dyed using the plants gathered throughout the year: a colourful frilled-edge linen cushion cover for spring; a hand-embroidered picnic blanket for summer; a hot water bottle cover for autumn; and a cosy patchwork bed quilt for winter.

I hope you enjoy coming on this seasonal journey, and that you experience the same excitement I felt when I first discovered the fascinating world of seasonal plant dyeing!

chapter one: harvesting plants

It's important that plants are harvested at the best time for producing good dye results and in such a way that maintains the health of the plant, ensuring future harvests, while respecting the environment in which they grow

ABOVE In the peak growing season it's possible to harvest flowers from annual plants every other day.

LEFT flowers should be harvested before they start to look tired and go brown. This will ensure that you get the best colour result from them.

BULBS

Dye can be extracted from both the flower of the bulb and the bulb itself. To harvest the flower of bulb, cut off the fresh flower head and leave the stem, allowing the goodness from the stem to travel back down into the bulb, giving the plant energy to flower again next season. Dyes that are made from the bulb itself are best harvested once they've finished flowering and the foliage has died back. Lift the whole plant and separate half of the bulbs for dyeing, and plant the other half back in the ground, making sure you replant a mixture of older and newer bulbs, because the newer bulbs can take a few years to flower.

ANNUALS

Annual flowers (plants that perform their entire life cycle from seed, to flower, to seed again within a single growing season) thrive on being deadheaded, and the more frequently the older flowers are removed, the faster the new ones grow. Typically, annuals will flower from late spring through to early autumn and can be deadheaded during this time. Instead of simply cutting off the flower you want to harvest, it's best to cut just above a newer bud that's lower down the stem. This will avoid leaving a length of stem on the plant that will start to die back and possibly harbour disease. In the peak growing season, flowers can be harvested every other day.

Annuals that are grown to use the roots for dyeing should be harvested at the peak of the season, when the plant is at its largest. The whole plant should be lifted and the roots separated for dyeing. As the season begins to come to an end, it's a good idea to stop deadheading to enable the flowers to fully mature and develop seeds, which can be saved for sowing the following year.

PERENNIALS

Perennials (plants that persist for many growing seasons) with roots that are used for dyeing are best lifted from the ground and divided in half.

Yarrow plants like full sun but they'll grow in nearly any soil and will happily self-seed. To harvest for dyeing, simply cut off the whole flower heads, leaving the foliage to allow more flowers to grow.

St John's wort can be picked off as it blooms, and stored in the freezer until enough has been collected to use for dye.

One half of the roots can be saved for dyeing; the other half of the plant can be planted back into the ground, to grow again for the following year's harvest. This is best done between late autumn and early spring, when the ground is workable and not frozen or wet.

Perennials that have flowers or foliage that's used for dyeing should be harvested as the new flowers or foliage emerge. They can also be divided between late autumn and early spring to create more plants and a larger harvest in the future. To ensure it has enough energy to grow again, make sure you cut from different sections of the plant and don't harvest more than half of the plant at a time. By cutting the plant, you'll encourage lots of new growth, so it's important to make sure you harvest foliage after all risk of frost has passed. Flowers can be harvested at any time.

SHRUBS

The best time to harvest from any given shrub depends on what time of year it flowers, if it's evergreen, and whether you want to dye from the flowers or the foliage. Flowers are best harvested when freshly opened and before they start to go brown, so pick them as soon as they appear, no matter the time of year. If you're dyeing from a shrub that flowers during the winter months, be especially mindful that many insects depend on the nectar as an energy source throughout the colder times of the year. As a general rule, summer and autumn flowering shrubs should be pruned in late winter or early spring, so there's plenty of time for the next season's growth to develop and produce flowers.

Shrubs that flower from later winter to early spring should be pruned after they've finished flowering, as they normally flower on the previous year's growth. This gives the plant time to put on enough growth during the warmer months for the following year's flowers. Most evergreen shrubs don't need annual pruning, so it's best to harvest the foliage from these from late spring through to early autumn, when there's no risk of frost. This means that any new growth as a result of pruning and harvesting will not be damaged.

HARVESTING PLANTS FROM THE WILD

When it comes to harvesting plants from the wild for dyeing, it's important to forage with thought and care to the environment. The key to doing this is to take a small number of plants from each area, while making sure the plant isn't a protected or rare variety. Don't harvest a plant unless you're

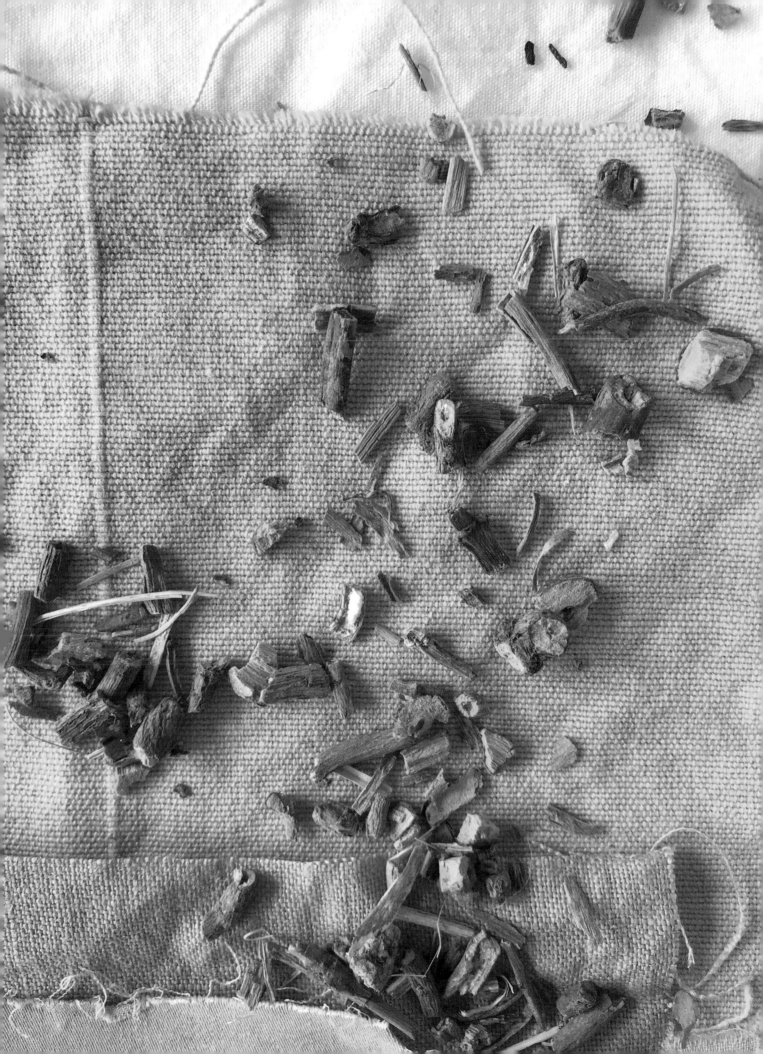

Harvests of things that dry well naturally without spoiling such as bark, lichen, pine cones, and leaves like bay and eucalyptus should be left to dry out before storing in paper bags or cardboard boxes.

certain of what you're picking (it's not uncommon for toxic or harmful plants to look very similar to their harmless twin). If you're unsure, research the plant first. Bark and alder/pine cones make great dyes, but harvest these from the ground, if possible, and never pull off bark directly from a tree trunk. Look out for fallen branches, pieces of bark, and lichen littering the floor after a storm, as these all produce fantastic dye material.

Many areas are public land and can be foraged by anyone, but make sure this is the case before you begin, and check that the plant isn't protected under the Wildlife and Countryside Act (1981) or your country's equivalent law. Respect the environment you're harvesting, be careful not to damage surrounding plants, and keep an eye out for any animals that might be hiding.

As well as harvesting from your own garden and foraging plants from the wild, keep your eyes open for neighbours who might be pruning shrubs or felling trees that you can take cuttings from to use as dye.

Finally, remember other plant foragers. You might not be the only person in your area who'll be delighted to stumble across a patch of goldenrod or yarrow growing in the wild, so leave plenty for someone else to discover!

STORING PLANT HARVESTS

Some dyes require a large quantity of flowers and unless you have lots of the same plant growing in your garden, it's unlikely that you'll be able to harvest enough at one time. Some plants need to be harvested and then stored before they can be used to make a dye. The freezer is the best place to store the majority of plants because it prevents them from going brown and losing their colour. Make sure you wash plants thoroughly to remove any dirt and bugs, which can discolour the dye, and place them in clearly labelled bags or pots in the freezer. It's helpful to put the harvest date and the location of where they were harvested on the bag.

Plants can be used straight from the freezer, but it's best to keep those harvested from different areas for separate dye batches, just in case the dye is altered by factors such as the soil the plant was grown in, or if the plants are similar looking but different varieties. Older and newer harvests can be used in the same dye batch, but bear in mind that the longer the plants have been stored in the freezer, the more likely it is they'll have started to degrade and may produce less vivid colours.

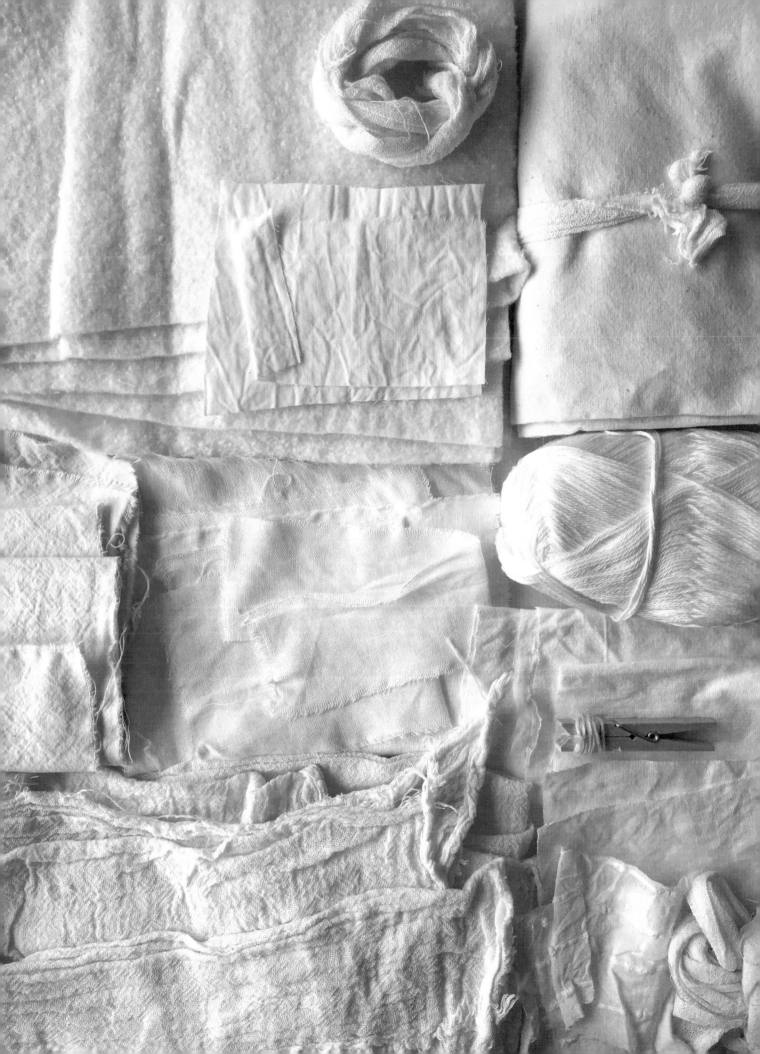

chapter two: choosing fabrics

Before dyeing, it's important to know the composition of your fabric, because this will affect how it absorbs a dye and help you understand how to care for your plant-dyed fabric properly, keeping it looking its best

ABOVE Walnut shells have been used to dye this fabric and wool a light brown shade. Plant colours will vary from batch to batch, so it's a good idea to ensure you have enough of a plant for the whole of the project you want to complete.

LEFT Fabrics can be split into three groups: synthetic fibres, semi-synthetic fibres and natural fibres (which can be split into two groups: plant sources and animal sources).

SYNTHETIC FIBRES

Synthetic fabrics are those that are considered man-made because they're manufactured, rather than harvested, and are often made from petrochemical sources. The most common synthetic fabrics are polyester, nylon and acrylic, which come from oil or coal. Although synthetic fabrics all have good aspects to them, such as being recyclable (polyester), warm to wear (nylon and acrylic) and quick drying (acrylic and polyester), they don't give the best colour results with plant dyes.

Additionally, when using plants dyes, it's assumed that you're taking a step to be more in touch with nature and the environment, so it would be more in keeping to work with fabrics that have the least affect on the environment during their production process.

SEMI-SYNTHETIC FIBRES

Semi-synthetic fibres, such as rayon, modal and bamboo, are made from raw natural materials like wood and seaweed, and modified by chemical processes to make the finished fabric. The processes used to create semi-synthetic fabrics mean that they have few or no characteristics that relate to the natural source from which they're derived, but, in my experience, all these fabrics can be dyed successfully with plant dyes.

Rayon

Rayon is made mainly from wood pulp that's chemically treated, before being forced through a spinneret (a bit like a shower head) to create long fibres that are spun into yarn and then woven into fabric. There are many types of rayon and it can imitate a variety of fabrics like linen, wool, silk and cotton, and is used for a wide range of clothing. It's prone to shrinking and usually needs to be hand washed or dry cleaned.

Modal

Modal is most commonly made from fibres of the beech tree, and is manufactured in the same way as rayon. It's stronger than rayon when it's wet and has a similar feel to cotton. Breathable and absorbent, it's most often used in items that benefit from being soft and comfortable to wear, and stand up to regular washing on a gentle cycle – such as pyjamas, underwear, activewear and bedsheets.

Bamboo

Bamboo fabric is often marketed as sustainable and environmentally friendly, because bamboo plants have a fast rate of growth and don't require pesticides. Many people will be surprised to learn that bamboo is actually manufactured in the same way as rayon and modal. In fact, many fabrics that are made from bamboo are simply labelled as rayon, rather than bamboo. Once it has been turned into a fabric (which is creamy coloured in its natural and unbleached state), bamboo is able to wick moisture away from the wearer's skin. Bamboo fabric tends to be very soft, and is most often made into bamboo silk or stretchy, soft soft cotton. Washing bamboo at high temperatures can shrink it, but otherwise it's an easy to care for fabric.

NATURAL FIBRES

Natural fibres can be split into two groups: those that come from animal sources, such as silk, raw silk, wild silk, sheep's wool, mohair, angora and cashmere; and those that come from plant sources, such as cotton, linen, hemp and raffia. It's often assumed that natural fabrics are kinder to the environment than synthetic or semi-synthetic fabrics, but this depends on how the plants have been grown (e.g. organically or not), how the animals that provide the raw wool and silk for fabrics are treated, and what chemicals are used during the manufacturing process.

ANIMAL-SOURCED NATURAL FIBRES

Animal-source fabrics, such as silk and wool, take up plant dyes easily due to the protein in the fibre. They're a great choice for achieving rich, deep colours, because they tend to absorb the dye well.

Silk

Silk is most commonly obtained from the cocoons of silkworms (caterpillars of the domestic silkmoth), which are reared in captivity and feed on leaves from the white mulberry tree, resulting in silk that's pale in colour. Once the silkworm has spun its cocoon, it's heated and then soaked in boiling water to soften the silk fibres, allowing it to be unwound more easily. This produces a continuous thread that can be up to a mile long. Several of these delicate, fine threads are spun together, before it's woven into silk fabric. The prism-like structure of the silk fibre allows the cloth to refract light at different angles in a way that can't be mimicked by synthetic or semi-synthetic fabrics. For such a delicate feeling fabric, silk is surprisingly strong and, historically, it had many commercial uses. Its high absorbency means that silk is comfortable to wear in warm weather. It's also breathable, so is commonly used for a variety of clothing, particularly formal wear due to its luxurious appearance and good drape. Most items made from silk require careful washing with cool water and a gentle soap to avoid shrinking or altering the texture of the fabric.

Peace Silk

Peace silk is produced slightly differently from normal silk. The larvae are allowed to mature into moths and make their own way out of their silk cocoons (or the cocoons are cut to enable the moths to escape), which is seen as a more humane way to obtain the threads. As the silk worms emerge from the cocoons, the long fibre of silk will break, which means peace silk isn't as smooth and silky as normal silk, and will often have characterful nubs on the surface. Despite the difference in texture, peace silk still requires the same careful washing as normal silk.

Wild Silk

Wild silk refers to the way in which the silkworms are raised, not the process of extracting the silk fibre. The silkworms that produce wild silk live outside and in less controlled conditions than the silkworms that are reared in captivity. This, along with the fact that the silk is usually harvested after the moths have left their cocoons, results in a fabric that has a similar texture to peace silk. Because the silkworms eat a varied diet, the silk that they produce can vary in colour from cream through golden colours to browns. Again, wild silk needs to be washed carefully in cool water with a gentle soap.

Wool

Wool is obtained when sheep are sheared and the fleece is cleaned, combed into long thin strips and then spun into a yarn. This yarn is either wound into balls of wool for knitters to use or transferred to cones so that it can be used on industrial knitting machines. This is the process that all the animal fibres listed below go through. Wool is a protein fibre and naturally hydrophilic (it can absorb water), which means that it takes plant dye extremely well. The appearance of wool can vary, depending on which area of the sheep the wool is taken from, but all wool is warm and waterproof. Although white is the most common colour for sheep wool (this has been selectively bred into sheep over years because it makes the dyeing process easier), it's possible to buy wool in a variety of natural colours. Due to its thermal properties, wool is a popular choice for cold-weather clothing, such as jumpers, gloves and hats. When caring for items made from wool, it's important not to subject them to high temperatures, as this will cause them to shrink and felt.

Mohair

Mohair comes from the hair of the angora goat (not to be confused with the angora rabbit, below) when it's sheared twice a year. Fabrics made from mohair remain cool in the summer and warm in the winter and it's often blended with other fibres to give them a luscious sheen. Typically, the natural colour of mohair is white, and it's frequently used in more luxurious

Plant-dyed fabrics and wools have a wonderful way of coordinating and matching together, such as the earthy tones of this wool dyed with dahlia flowers, walnut shells, yarrow flowers and chamomile flowers.

knitted items such as jumpers, hats and accessories. It requires very gentle washing in a cool temperature to prevent it felting and shrinking.

Angora
Angora comes from the long-haired fluffy angora rabbit and the fur is pulled out as it moults. Angora is an expensive fur because the rabbits have to be groomed regularly to prevent their fur from matting and felting. Angora is known for being very soft, lightweight and warm, and for having a halo of fluff surrounding the yarn. It's quite often blended with other wools when sold as knitting yarn, because pure angora can felt easily and is difficult to work with. Angora rabbits naturally have coats in a wide variety of colours, ranging from white through to brown and black. It's best to hand wash angora to avoid damaging the soft fibres.

Cashmere
Cashmere comes from the long hair on the necks of the cashmere goat and is collected when the goat naturally sheds its winter coat. It's finer, lighter, softer and stronger than sheep's wool, which makes it more expensive. The natural colour of cashmere is white, brown and grey, and it's typically used for luxury knitwear. Cashmere should always be hand washed in cool water.

PLANT-SOURCED NATURAL FIBRES
Fabrics that are made from plants often have a reputation for being difficult to colour with plant dyes, but, with a little help, they absorb colours really well and give excellent results.

Cotton
Cotton comes from the cotton plant (*Gossypiym*), and the fibres grow as creamy-white fluffy balls on the plant, which look and feel very similar to the cotton wool balls you buy in the chemist. The fibre is spun into thread and used to make soft, breathable clothing such as knitted jersey T-shirts and woven cotton bedding. Most items made from cotton can withstand repeated washing at high temperatures.

Linen
Linen fabric is made from the flax plant that's harvested and dried before the fibres are treated and then spun into yarn. Compared to cotton, the production process of linen is more labour intensive, which is why linen is typically more expensive. Linen is very absorbent (which means it takes

Triangles of linen, dyed with eucalyptus leaves, rosemary leaves, ivy leaves, alkanet roots and alder cones, ready for a patchwork project.

plant dyes well) and clothing that's made from linen will keep the wearer feeling cool and fresh. The natural colours of linen include cream, grey and pale brown (pure white linen is achieved by bleaching the fabric during the manufacturing process). It should be washed using a cool water cycle in a washing machine and will get softer and more absorbent with each wash.

Hemp

Hemp comes from the *Cannabis Sativa* plant. Once harvested, the woody centre of the plant is separated from the fibres. The plant grows well without pesticides or other chemical intervention, meaning that in comparison to other fibres such as cotton, it's more environmentally friendly to produce. Hemp has a texture that's similar to linen and it's often blended with other fibres to create fabrics that are strong and durable. Hemp's natural cream colour means that it needs less (if any) bleaching in the manufacturing process to make it light enough for successful dyeing. Hemp is absorbent and good at screening out ultraviolet rays, which means it takes dyes well and is less likely the fade compared with other fabrics. Hemp should be washed using cool water.

Raffia

Raffia is made from the membrane on the underside of palm tree leaves. This membrane is taken off to reveal a long thin fibre that can be used as a natural string to make baskets or garden twine. The natural colour of raffia is a cream. It dyes well, but care must to be taken to avoid it getting tangled in the dyeing process. Raffia should be washed using cool water.

A NOTE ON FABRIC COMPOSITION

When buying fabrics (particularly online), double check the composition, as quite often the name is used to describe the properties of the fabric rather than the actual fibre that it's made from. For instance, I've found fabrics that are listed as 'silk', but on closer inspection they're polyester or a blend of different fibres (sometimes with a little silk) that have a soft, smooth and 'silky' feel. Again, a polyester and cotton blend is sometimes labelled as just cotton.

Before using a plant dye to colour a fabric it is a good idea to put a small piece of the fabric into the dye pot to see how well it absorbs the dye.

NATURAL FABRIC COLOUR AND DYE RESULTS

Many plant and animal source fabrics have a wide range of natural colours, from almost white to very dark greys and black, which either enhance or dull a plant dye. Fabrics that are naturally cream give a wonderful warm tone to plant dyes, and those that are grey can give a more vintage, worn-in feel to a colour.

Fabrics that have previously been dyed a strong or bright colour may prove tricky to successfully over-dye and the resulting colour is normally made from a mix of the existing colour of the fabric and the colour of the dye that's been used. For example, when coloured with a yellow dye, a piece of fabric that was originally red will take on more of an orangey colour, rather than becoming yellow.

It's worth experimenting with pale coloured fabrics that have a print on them, because often the pale-coloured background successfully colours with the plant dye but the print does not, which can give interesting results.

FABRIC WEIGHT AND DYE RESULTS

The weight (or thickness) of a fabric will affect the colour achieved with plant dyes. Velvet can produce intense colour results because it's a densely woven, relatively heavy-weight fabric. If you cut a 1cm square section of velvet and pulled it apart thread by thread, you'd find a much higher number of threads than a lightweight, thinner fabric such as a cotton muslin, which will produce paler colour results. Before using a plant dye it's a good idea to put a small piece of the fabric into the dye pot to see how well it absorbs the dye.

chapter three: tools

The wonderful thing about dyeing with plants is that no expensive equipment is required. All you need to get started are the right plants growing in your garden – or places where you can forage – and a few old pot and pans

It's really important to keep your dyeing utensils separate from those used for cooking. Although many dye plants are harmless, there are some that are toxic, especially when they're heated.

The things you need to begin your plant-dyeing journey:

1. LARGE SAUCEPAN or pot that can fit safely on your hob. The larger the pan, the more fabric that can be dyed at once, but remember that very large pans can get extremely heavy when filled with liquid. I use an aluminium pot because aluminium acts a little like an alum mordant (fixative), making the colours brighter. You can also experiment with using an iron pot to sadden the colours slightly.

2. WOODEN SPOONS for stirring the dye. It's important to use a wooden spoon, especially with dyes that require constant stirring, so the heat doesn't transfer to the spoon and become too hot to hold. I recommend having a selection of wooden spoons, one for each colour range (reds, greens, yellows), so that any dye that's soaked into the spoon won't spoil another colour.

3. SIEVE/COLANDER AND MUSLIN CLOTHS OR OLD TEA TOWELS to use when separating the dye from the plants once any colour has been extracted. The fabric is placed on top of the sieve or colander to catch small bits of plants. The fabric can then be squeezed to wring out every last bit of dye from the plants before it's composted.

4. SPARE BOWL to pour the dye into as it's separated from the pieces of plant.

5. APRON AND RUBBER GLOVES to protect you and your clothing. Concentrated plant dyes quickly stain fabrics (and hands!), and it's easy to not notice splashes when you're busy dyeing.

It's really important to keep your dyeing utensils separate from those used for cooking. Although many dye plants are harmless, some are toxic, especially when they're heated and concentrated.

chapter four: soya milk

Mordants, such as soya milk, are used to achieve bright, vivid colours, as well as helping dye to stick to fabric. Depending on the mordant, it can be added to the fabric either before, during, or after the dyeing process

In all of my dyeing projects I choose to use soya milk as a mordant, as it's safe and chemical-free. Soya milk acts as a binder to lock the colour pigments into the fabric as the protein molecules in the milk change over time and go from being soluble in water to being insoluble which is why it helps to seal the colour to the fabric.

One of the most common mordants to use with plant dyes is alum, which is bought in a powder or crystal form and is mixed with water to soak the fabric before it's dyed. Other mordants include gall nuts, rhubarb leaves, iron, tin, copper, chrome, juniper needles and sumac leaves, but some of these are considered to be toxic and should be used with caution.

Not all plant dyes will require a mordant to help them successfully dye fabric, as some plant dyes are rich in tannins that help them to be colour fast. However, I would recommend mordanting all fabrics in soya milk before dyeing them, because soya milk can improve the colour results and help the dye stick to the fabric. Soya milk also has the benefit of not altering or changing the feel and texture of fibres, unlike other mordants which can damage fabric if used at too high a temperature or in too concentrated a dose.

HOW TO MORDANT FABRIC WITH SOYA MILK

1. Even if it's new, fabric should be washed before it's mordanted. Processes that are used in fabric manufacture sometimes leave a coating on the fabric that could affect how well the fabric absorbs a dye. It's often recommended to scour fabrics by boiling them with soda ash and repeating the process several times, but I find that a wash with some natural laundry detergent cleans the fabrics well enough for them to be successfully dyed.

2. After it has been washed, place the damp fabric into a bucket and add soya milk and water in a ratio of roughly two parts water to one part soya milk. Stir the bucket to make sure the fabric is coated evenly in the soya milk mixture and leave it to soak for 48 hours. Make sure it's kept somewhere cool to prevent the mixture from curdling (if this happens then the fabric will need to be washed and the process started again) and stir it a few times during the 48 hours.

3. When the fabric has finished soaking, squeeze off the excess soya milk and put the fabric in a washing machine on a spin cycle to get rid of any additional moisture. This will prevent the soya milk mixture from running down the fabric when it's hung to dry, which would cause patchy results.

4. Hang the fabric to air dry and then leave it to 'rest' for a minimum of a week before it's dyed. This rest enables the protein molecules in the soya milk to go from being soluble in water to being insoluble, causing it to become a binder between the fabric and the dye.

chapter five: dyeing basics

For the best colour results, each plant has specific instructions later on in this book, but below is a general guide to the process involved in extracting colour from plants, dyeing fabric and storing dyes

Extracting the colour from the plants correctly will ensure that you create vivid, brightly coloured dyes.

EXTRACTING THE COLOUR FROM PLANTS

1. Leave harvested plants outside for a few hours to allow insects to crawl away before the plant goes into the dye pot. Unless it's particularly muddy, there's no need to wash the plants before extracting the dye.

2. To make the dye, plants should be placed into the dye pot with some cold water and gradually heated to a gentle simmer. Plant dyes generally shouldn't be allowed to boil, and this is particularly true with delicate flowers, because they'll end up being cooked, which causes the dye to go brown. Plants just need to be heated enough so that the colour starts to be released.

3. Plants are usually left to simmer very gently for a while in the water, before the heat is turned off, and then they're left to sit in the dye for anything from a few hours to several days. The amount of time that the plants are left changes according to which plant is being used. Some plants go through several different colour stages and will produce different colours depending on how long they're left in the dye pot.

4. Once all of the dye has been extracted from the plants, the dye is strained to get rid of any small pieces of plant. This is an important stage and one that shouldn't be left out, as any small pieces of plant left in the dye can cause patches of darker or different colours on fabric. If you're dyeing yarn of any kind then the small pieces of plant tend to get tangled up in the yarn and are fiddly to get out. To avoid this, place a muslin cloth or an old tea towel on a sieve over a large glass bowl or saucepan and pour the dye through. The fabric will catch any small pieces of plant and can be squeezed to get any remaining dye out of them. The plants can then be composted and the piece of fabric washed, ready to use for the next dye project.

5. Before pouring the dye back in, the dye pot to should be washed to remove any pieces of plant that could spoil the fabric (see above point).

DYEING THE FABRIC

1. Lower the fabric into the dye in the pot, then slowly heat it to a gentle simmer. It's important to make sure that there's enough dye in the pot for the fabric to be fully submerged under the water level. If needed, add a little extra water to top it up. Fabric can be put into the dye pot when it's dry or wet, but you may find that you get better results on larger pieces of fabric if they're damp before they go into the pot because this helps the fabric to absorb the colour more evenly. The fabric should be stirred for a minute or so when it's first put into the dye to help the colour to distribute, and to avoid any undyed patches resulting from folds in the fabric. Generally, the fabric should be simmered for about 30 minutes before the heat is turned off and it's left to soak.

2. Fabric left in the dye pot for any length of time should be stirred occasionally and checked that it's all still submerged under the water level of the pot (the fabric can be weighed down with a couple of wooden spoons if necessary). This will prevent any fabric that's sitting above the water line from oxidising, which can cause it to turn a different or darker colour.

3. Once the fabric has been dyed the required colour and the dye is cool, it can be lifted out of the pot and the excess moisture squeezed out. It is a good idea to do this over the dye pot so that the excess dye drips back into the pot. Many dye pots can be used multiple times, producing paler (and sometimes even different) colours with each subsequent use. Make sure you squeeze rather than wring the fabric to prevent it from becoming misshapen – fabrics can be easily manipulated out of shape when they're wet.

4. Ideally, fabric should be dried outside over a lawn or a similar area that won't matter if the occasional splash of dye gets onto it. If the weather isn't suitable for dying outside and the fabric needs to be dried indoors, do so on a drying rack that's placed over an old bath towel on the floor to soak up any drips. In both cases, it's important to make sure the fabric is dried away from direct heat sources and out of direct sunlight, because this can lighten or fade the colour.

5. Once the fabric is dry, it should be ironed with a dry iron (using a heat setting suitable for the fabric) to set the colour and help prevent the colour running when it's washed.

6. Next, the fabric should be washed on a cool cycle in the washing machine using a gentle and natural laundry detergent to get rid of any excess dye.

7. Lastly, the fabric can be hung to dry for a final time, again out of direct sunlight and heat.

Although this book gives set times for extracting the colour from the plants and dyeing fabric, these are just guidelines, as there are many factors that can affect the colour you achieve. A good way to test how the dye is being extracted from a plant is to dip a glass into the dye pot and get an indication of the colour. The dye liquid can look slightly darker (or even a slightly different shade) than how it will look on fabric. To test the progression of dye on fabric, lift a corner of the fabric out of the dye pot and squeeze out the excess moisture. Wet fabric is always a few shades darker than dry fabric but, otherwise, this is the best way to see the colour on the fabric.

DYEING WOOL

The principles of dyeing wool are the same as the normal dye process but with a few exceptions. To help the absorption of the soya milk and dye particles, wool benefits from being soaked in water first. A ball, skein or hank of wool needs to be unwound so that it will dye evenly. Wind it into a loop and tie it loosely in several places to keep it together. Extra care should be taken throughout the dyeing and mordanting process to make sure it doesn't get too tangled, and squeezing the wool dry rather than wringing it will prevent it from felting. Whereas fabric can be washed in the washing machine, a ball of wool needs to be hand washed, and the ironing stage at the end of the dyeing process should be skipped.

STORING AND DISPOSING OF THE DYES

One of the easiest ways to store plant dyes is in airtight glass jars that have been thoroughly cleaned and sterilised to help prevent mould from growing. These jars should then be kept somewhere out of direct heat and sunlight. Another option is to keep them in the freezer either in glass jars (make sure to leave an expansion gap) or in pots. Dye can either be poured into jars straight from the dye pot (let the dye cool completely first) or concentrated so that it takes up less space when it's stored. To concentrate the dye, simmer it in the pan with the lid off to evaporate some of the liquid, before letting it cool down and pouring it into a jar. Remember that dyes that have been concentrated will need to have more liquid added to them when it comes to using them.

Since the methods used in this book are chemical-free, any leftover dye can be disposed of by pouring it directly onto your compost bin or flowerbed, using it to water your plants, or pouring it down the sink. If the dye still seems to have a lot of colour particles left in it and you don't want to store it or use it again, then it's a good idea to add a little extra water when disposing of it.

CARING FOR PLANT-DYED COLOURS

The best way to care for plant-dyed fabrics is to wash them in cool water using a gentle and natural soap, drying them and storing them out of direct sunlight. The great thing about dyeing your own fabrics is that if they do fade, it's always possible to dye them again!

chapter six: modifiers

Modifiers alter the colour of a dye and they're usually used after the fabric has been dyed. Sometimes a modifier can also double as a mordant, which means that it helps the dye to stick, as well as changing its colour

Using iron with ivy leaves has turned this fabric from pale to dark grey. Iron works very quickly so don't leave the fabric in the liquid for long.

Some plant dyes are pH-sensitive, and modifiers can work to alter the pH of a dye to create a dramatic colour change. Modifiers that are used to shift the pH of a dye to acid are lemon juice, vinegar and citric acid; and modifiers that are used to shift the pH of a dye to alkali are chalk (calcium carbonate), ammonia and wood ash. Be wary when soaking animal source fabrics in a solution that's too alkaline as it can damage the fabric.

IRON
When iron is used as a modifier, it dulls colours and turns them darker. This can have very interesting results as it can turn pinks to purples and yellows to oranges. It's a good idea to keep a separate dye pot specifically for using iron, as it can leave a residue that will affect other dye projects. To use iron as a modifier, you can either use iron crystals (ferrous sulphate) or make your own iron water, which is my preferred method.

IRON WATER RECIPE
To make your own iron water you'll need a glass jar with a lid, water, vinegar and small rusty objects such as nails. Place the rusty objects into the jar and fill it with two parts water and one part vinegar, covering the objects. Over a few weeks the liquid in the jar will gradually turn orange and then eventually to a dark grey. It can be used by either adding a small amount of it to the dye, or mixing with water and soaking the fabric after it has been dyed. Iron works very quickly so the fabric won't need to be in the liquid for long. The same rusty objects can be used over and over - the pot just needs to be topped up with more water and vinegar as it's used, but don't try adding rusty objects directly to the dye pot, as this will result in patchy, uneven results.

COPPER
Copper saddens and dulls colours. Copper modifiers that are available to buy are considered toxic so I'd recommend making your own copper water (in the same way as the iron water recipe) but this time using copper coins and bits of copper pipe.

chapter seven: spring

Spring is a wonderful time of year for harvesting plants, as the warmer days encourage plenty of fresh green growth, and leaves yield their brightest colours for the dye pot. Early spring is ideal for collecting plants for their roots, too, catching them while they're still dormant, before they start to grow again as the weather begins to get warmer

mint leaves

Mint is commonly found in domestic gardens. It's a vigorous plant that spreads by its roots underground, and produces a lemon yellow dye

Latin name: *Mentha* **Common name:** Mint

Type: Herbaceous perennial

Mint is a highly aromatic plant with bright green leaves and purple-white flowers. It does best in partial shade, but it needs regular watering to avoid wilting in the full sun of the day. If you have a mint plant in a pot that's more than a year old, you may find that when it starts to grow again in the spring, all of the growth is around the edge of the pot, with seemingly nothing in the middle. To remedy this, take the plant out of the pot, cut it in half, remove some of the excess older roots and re-pot the two halves in separate pots in fresh compost.

Rather than growing mint from seed, you can easily take cuttings from existing plants to increase the number of plants you have:
1. Cut about 10cm from the top growth of the plant and remove the lower leaves, leaving two pairs.
2. Cut the stem just below a leaf node (the point on the stem where the leaves are growing) and place the cutting in a glass of water, making sure that the top two pairs of leaves are above the water level. You can put several cuttings into one glass.
3. Leave the glass in a light place – such as a windowsill – and the stem should start to grow roots within a few weeks. Keep the water level topped up until a good root system has established before potting up the cutting in a pot of multi-purpose compost.

Mint leaves produce the brightest yellows when they're new, so they should be harvested as soon as there are enough leaves for you to make your dye. Regular cutting and harvesting of the plant throughout spring and early summer will encourage it to put on more fresh growth – simply grab a handful of stems and cut them off, leaving 10cm of growth from the base of the plant.

Mint leaf dye recipe

Colour: Bright lemon yellow

You will need: 10 to 15 large handfuls of freshly cut mint (both leaves and stems). Compared to other dye plants, you'll need significantly more mint leaves to create a strong enough dye to produce a vibrant colour.

Making the dye
Put the mint in the dye pot with enough water to cover it and simmer gently for 10 minutes before turning off the heat. Leave the mint soaking for a day, during which time bring the water to a simmer and then turn it off again several times to encourage the colour out of the leaves.

Dyeing the fabric
Put the fabric in the dye and heat to a gentle simmer, leaving it at that temperature for 30 minutes to an hour. Turn off the heat and check the colour of the fabric. If you'd like to create a more intense colour, repeat the simmering and cooling process over the next few days.

Madder root dye recipe

Colour: Red

You will need: 100g dried madder roots; chalk (calcium carbonate).

Note: that calcium carbonate is different to chalkboard chalk, which is calcium sulphate.

If the madder roots have been freshly harvested, they should be washed and left to dry out for several weeks as the fresh roots tend to produce an orange colour, compared with the reds and pinks that can be produced from dried roots.

Making the dye
Finely chop the dried roots and put them to the dye pot, along with 5ltr water. Dissolve 10g chalk in a small amount of hot water before adding it to the dye pot. Heat the mixture for 2-3 hours, making sure it doesn't go above a simmer as the colour can be destroyed if the temperature gets too high.

Dyeing the fabric
Place the fabric in the dye, adding a little extra water if it's needed and heat it to a simmer for 2-3 hours before leaving it to soak overnight.

madder roots

The dye properties of the madder plant have been known from the early history – cloth dyed with madder has been found on ancient Egyptian mummies – with its roots producing rich pinky-red hues

Latin name: *Rubia tinctorum* **Common name:** Madder
Type: Evergreen perennial

Madder plants can grow up to 150cm tall and have long green leaves and small, pale yellow flowers that grow in clusters. Madder prefers well-drained soil in a sunny location and is often seen growing in rubble and neglected ground. It's a great plant to grow in your garden – with the right care and attention it will provide plant colour for years. The roots of the madder plant are used for dyeing. When grown from seed, the plant can't be used for dyeing for at least three years, so it's worth dedicating a specific area of the garden (or several large pots) to growing it. It spreads easily by its roots so should be separated from other plants to prevent it taking over your garden. It is the roots of the madder plant that produce a dye. Dividing them is a great way to increase the number of plants you have (and the amount of dye that you can make).

Plants can be divided at almost any time of year, providing the ground isn't waterlogged or frozen, and spring is the ideal time to harvest some of the roots.

To divide the plant, lift it gently using a fork or spade and shake off any soil from the roots. Using a spade, slice the root ball into three pieces. One third of this will be kept aside for dyeing, and the other two thirds can be replanted into the ground. An alternative to dividing the plants is to trim the whole root ball leaving about 15cm from the centre. This should be done in early spring, before the plant begins to grow again. I prefer the dividing method, as it gradually increases the number of plants and the size of the harvest each year. Replanting plenty of madder ensures that there are lots of roots to harvest in the future.

Bay leaf dye recipe

Colour: Reddish/pink/terracotta

You will need: 30 to 40 fresh young bay leaves.

Making the dye
Put the bay leaves in a pot with enough water to cover them and heat it to a simmer for 30 minutes. Turn off the heat and leave the leaves soaking for at least 12 hours. Stronger colours will be produced if they're left to soak for several days.

Dyeing the fabric
Place the fabric in the dye and heat to a gentle simmer for 30 minutes to one hour. Bay leaf dye is quite intense and tends to dye fabric quickly, so the fabric can be removed as soon as the dye is cool.

bay leaves

Used to make the laurel wreaths that emperors wore in ancient Rome, bay was considered to be good luck and guarded against evil spirits. Its soft spring leaves produce a terracotta-pink dye

Latin name: *Laurus nobilis* **Common name:** Bay
Type: Evergreen shrub that can grow to the size of a tree

Bay is a large, dense shrub that has aromatic leathery leaves that are used in cooking, and small, yellow-green flowers that appear in the spring. It's a common plant found in most garden centres but it can also be grown from seed. Freshly harvested seeds should be sown straight away, whereas dried (or bought) seeds need to be soaked for 24 hours before they're sown.

Most commonly found in domestic gardens, bay likes well-drained soil in a sunny but sheltered location. It's also happy growing in a container – just keep the roots wrapped up and warm during the winter months.

Once it gets going it can be left alone to do its own thing to grow to the size of a tree, providing a good habitat for small birds; or shaped into topiary, in which case it will need regular clipping (at least annually) to keep it in shape.

During the spring, pick the youngest leaves – which are easy to spot as they're a lighter colour and haven't yet turned leathery – as these provide the best colour. Leaves picked later in the year will provide a lovely rich beige colour, but the fresh spring leaves create the reddish-pink dye shown here. Just remember that if you're harvesting from a topiarised plant you should keep in mind the overall shape and not harvest all the leaves from the same place. Better still, use the clippings created from shaping the plant to make your dye.

Nettle top dye recipe

Colour: Bright to olive green

You will need: 3 to 4 large handfuls of freshly picked nettle leaves.

Making the dye
Put the leaves in the dye pot with just enough water to cover them. Slowly heat the pot until it begins to simmer gently and leave it like this for 10 minutes. Turn off the heat and let the leaves soak in the water as they release their colour. Soak the leaves in the water for several days, noting as the colour of the water gradually changes from yellow to green.

Dyeing the fabric
Place the fabric in the dye and heat the pot to a very gentle simmer for around 30 minutes and then leave the fabric to sit in the dye for 1-2 days. Be careful when heating the dye not to let it boil as the colour can spoil very quickly.

nettle tops

Nettles have historically been used in food, tea and traditional medicine, and when laying hens eat dried nettles it is said that their egg yolks turn a brighter yellow. The tops produce a vibrant green dye in spring

Latin name: *Urtica diocia* **Common name:** Stinging nettle

Type: Herbaceous perennial

Nettles grow from the beginning of spring and can reach up to two metres tall. They have bright yellow, spreading roots and the stems are covered with heart-shaped leaves. Widely regarded as an invasive weed, nettles like to grow in damp areas under the cover of other plants, but they're also found growing along the edges of paths as well as in domestic gardens.

If you want to introduce nettles into your garden to use as a dye plant, sow the seeds in a pot and keep it away from flowerbeds and other places that the roots can sneak into. Snip off any flowers as soon as you see them – they go to seed very quickly, and this will help prevent you ending up with a garden full of stinging nettles. Several species of butterfly larvae feed exclusively off the young leaves of nettles, so be extra careful when harvesting as they can hide between the leaves.

Nettles sting because of the tiny barbs on the underside of the leaves and on the stems, injecting a mixture of histamine, acetylcholine and serotonin which causes itching and swelling.

The best time to harvest the leaves from the plant is in the spring, choosing only the youngest leaves from the top of the plant, as these produce a wonderful bright green colour. As the plants get older throughout the year, the dye colour tends to dull and will produce more brown, beige and olive green shades.

Forsythia flower dye recipe

Colour: Golden/mustard yellow

You will need: four large handfuls of freshly picked (or frozen) forsythia flowers.

Making the dye
Put the flowers in the dye pot with enough water to cover them and heat them to a very gentle simmer before immediately turning off the heat. Leave them to soak in the water for a day.

Dyeing the fabric
Place the fabric in the dye and heat it to a very gentle simmer for 30 minutes to an hour, before turning off the heat and leaving the fabric to soak in the dye for several days until a rich colour develops. Be very careful not to let it boil, as the colour can spoil and turn to brown quickly.

forsythia flowers

One of the first brightly coloured shrubs to bloom every spring, forsythia's sunny yellow flowers stand out against a background of mostly grey, brown and green. It produces a muted yellow dye

Latin name: *Forsythia* **Common name:** Forsythia
Type: Deciduous shrub

Forsythia can grow up to 250cm tall and has bright yellow flowers in spring, followed by a covering of green leaves that last until the autumn. It's mostly found in gardens as feature shrubs or as an informal hedge along boundaries. It's very easy grow in all soil types, as long as it has a bit of sunshine.

In the spring, forsythia is covered in flowers, making it easy to harvest enough to dye with, while still leaving plenty on the plant for insects. Once it gets going, forsythia is so abundant with flowers that you can pick extra and freeze them to use for dyeing later in the year. The best time to pick the flowers is when they're still new and before they start to go brown. Flowers can simply be pulled off the plant gently – there's no need to cut them off.

Once the shrub has finished flowering, it should be pruned by cutting back the growth that has flowered to the shoots lower down. Forsythia will flower on the previous year's growth, so pruning soon after it's flowered will give it maximum time for new growth to develop.

spring project: linen cushion cover

This project combines all the colours of our spring plant dyes. Undyed linen is used for the base of the cushion cover; while green, red, pink, mustard and yellow dyed fabric adds a colourful frilled edging

Things you will need:

- 52cm x 52cm piece of medium-weight linen for the front of the cushion*, left undyed.

- Two 52cm x 37cm pieces of medium-weight linen for the back of the cushion, left undyed.

- Two 52cm x 15cm pieces of cotton calico for the lining of the cushion back, left undyed.

- Strips of medium-weight linen for the layered frilled edge. These should be 5cm wide and need to be at least 400cm long in total, split into several different lengths. These are dyed with nettle leaves, mint leaves, bay leaves, madder roots and forsythia flowers. Rather than cutting the strips, rip them to size. This will cause them to fray evenly so they look neater when they're made into the frilled edge.

- Unbleached cotton thread.

I've specified using a linen fabric for this project because it has a gorgeous texture and is perfect for the forthcoming warmer months. At 50cm square, this cushion cover is a generous size, making it great for bringing out to the garden on warm spring afternoons.

1. If you're backing your linen fabric with calico, then this should be done by pinning the two pieces of fabric and sewing them together, about 0.5cm from the edge to secure them in place.

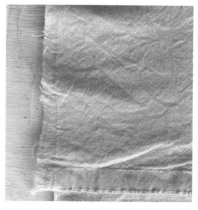

2. Sew the lining pieces to the rear of the cushion. Line up the longest edges of one of the lining pieces with one of the back pieces. With the right sides of the fabric facing each other, use a 1cm seam to stitch them together. Repeat with the other lining and back pieces.

3. Use an iron to press the seams open flat.

4. Fold the lining piece over and iron it so that the cushion back piece is folded over by a few millimetres. This will ensure the lining piece stays hidden when the cushion is finished. Repeat with the other lining and back piece. Overlap the two back cushion pieces by 22cm.

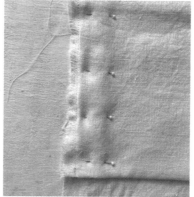

5. Make sure the edges that are sewn to the lining are facing each other. These will become the back of the cushion, so check that it's the same size as the front cushion piece. Alter the overlap if needed, and pin them in place. Stitch them 0.5cm from the edge and remove the pins.

6. The beauty of this cushion is that the arrangement of the linen strips is totally organic, so before you stitch the strips in place, lay them out along the edge of the cushion front piece and overlap and rearrange them until you're happy with how they look.

7. To attach the frill, line up the edge of a linen strip, making sure the right sides of the fabric are facing together and stitch them in place. Sew on each strip, overlapping them slightly.

8. Make slight tucks and gathers in the frill as you sew. Each time you finish sewing a strip, consider carefully the placement of the next one to ensure that the colours are equally balanced.

9. Once all of the strips have been sewn, place the cushion back and front right sides together and use a few pins to hold them in place. Stitch the pieces together, using a 1cm seam allowance.

10. Once you've finished sewing, carefully snip the ends of the corners, making sure you don't cut though the stitching, and turn the cushion the right way around.

If your linen fabric is too thin, then it can be backed with a piece of cotton calico fabric of the same size. This will prevent the coloured seams of the plant-dyed frill from showing through.

chapter eight: summer

Summer is a real hive of activity. Flowers can be harvested almost daily and stored until enough have been collected to make a dye. The early summer flowering plants such as lavender can be cut back after flowering and the foliage used for dyeing, whereas fresh woad leaves are abundant enough all through the season, enabling large amounts to be collected

buddleja flowers

Commonly known as the 'butterfly bush', buddleja is a sturdy plant with attractive conical flowers on an arching bush of silvery-green foliage. The purple flower heads produce a sunshine yellow dye in summer

Latin name: *Buddleja* **Common name:** Butterfly bush

Type: Deciduous perennial that can grow to tree size

Buddleja flower dye recipe

Colour: Bright yellow

You will need: 10 to 20 buddleja flower heads.

Making the dye
Put the whole flower heads in a dye pot with enough water to cover them and heat them on a very gentle heat for 10 minutes, making sure the water doesn't get too hot. Leave the flowers soaking overnight so that the water turns a lovely yellow colour.

Dyeing the fabric
Place the fabric in the dye and heat it to a very low simmer for 30 minutes to an hour. Leave the fabric in the dye to cool before removing it.

Buddleja have fantastic, highly scented flowers that cover the plant during the summer and autumn. The large purple flowers are great for attracting butterflies (hence the nickname 'butterfly bush') and are commonly spotted in domestic gardens, as well as in a variety of places where they've self-seeded. I once spotted it growing out of the wall of a house, two stories high!

Buddleja can be grown from seed and will normally flower in its first year or can be bought as a plant, which will give you more flowers, more quickly. I have a lovely dwarf variety that grows in a pot in my front garden – perfect if you don't have much space but would still like to grow it as a dye plant in your garden.

Although they're fairly long lasting, buddleja flowers tend to go brown pretty quickly, so are best used when they're freshly opened. You can encourage more flowers by regularly deadheading the plant, removing the fresh flowers and storing the cut flower heads in the freezer until enough have been collected to use for dyeing. Deadheading the plant will also encourage lots of new flowers. Buddleja should be pruned every year in the spring to encourage lots of new growth (and flowers) later on in the year.

goldenrod flowers

Goldenrod's fluffy plumes pop up all over the summer landscape, and its flowers produce a greenish yellow dye. Often accused of causing hay fever, it's also considered to be a sign of good luck

Latin name: *Solidago* **Common name:** Goldenrod

Type: Deciduous perennial

Popular as a cut flower in floristry, goldenrod can grow up to a metre tall and has narrow green leaves and clumps of bright yellow flowers from late summer through to the early autumn. It provides nectar for migrating butterflies and bees, encouraging them to remain in the area and pollinate crops.

Goldenrod likes full sun, well-drained, sandy soil and is commonly found growing in open areas, such as meadows and waste ground. It's a really easy plant to grow in the garden: if it's planted in the right conditions, then it needs very little attention.

To harvest the plant, cut the flowers off and leave the stalks, which should encourage new side shoots (and more flowers) to appear. The best time to harvest the flowers for dye is when they're fully open but still new and not turning brown. Using the plant before the flowers are fully open will result in a much greener shade, as will putting the leaves and the stems in the dye pot along with the flowers.

Goldenrod flower dye recipe

Colour: Greenish yellow

You will need: 20 to 25 flower tops.

Making the dye
Remove the flowers from the stems and put them in the dye pot with enough water to cover them, gently simmer for 10 minutes and then turn off the heat. The best colour is achieved if the goldenrod is left to soak in the water, rather than being heated for too long, so leave it in the pot for 1-2 days, until the water turns a yellowy-green colour.

Dyeing the fabric
Place the fabric in the dye with a little extra water if it's needed and heat the dye to a simmer for 10 minutes. Turn off the heat and leave the fabric to soak for a few days before removing it.

lavender leaves

A versatile herb, lavender's flowers are used in traditional herbal medicine, aromatherapy and essential oils. It's used to reduce stress and soothe away aching muscles, as well as being great for attracting bees and butterflies. Lavender leaves produce a soft grey dye

Latin name: *Lavandula* **Common name:** Lavender
Type: Evergreen shrub

Lavender has grey-green, highly scented foliage and spikes of aromatic flowers in the summer. The flowers are most commonly purple, but they can sometimes be pale pink or white. The plant will produce a grey dye no matter the colour of the flowers. Found in domestic gardens, lavender likes full sun and well-drained soil. It should be pruned yearly to keep it in shape, and to prevent it from becoming too leggy, with bare stems at the base.

The ideal time to prune lavender is in the late summer after it has flowered. This will give it plenty of time to put on new growth before the cooler months begin, and will help it to flower earlier in the following year. Remove the flower stalks (these can be composted) and take off about 2.5cm of the current year's foliage growth, which can be used for dyeing. Growth that's harvested during the summer months usually produces a grey dye; leaves collected from early spring growth normally produces beige and light brown dyes.

Lavender is rarely grown from seed and is mostly available to buy as plants. Alternatively, it grows well from cuttings. The best time to take cuttings from lavender plants is in the summer. Cut soft new growth that hasn't flowered yet and remove the lowest few sets of leaves so that there's a length of bare stem left. Insert the cuttings around the edge of a pot filled with gritty compost and leave them in a warm place. Keep the soil moist and they should root in about five to six weeks.

Lavender leaf dye recipe

Colour: Grey

You will need: 2 to 3 large handfuls of lavender leaves. Don't worry too much if the occasional stem gets in the dye pot.

Making the dye
Put the lavender leaves in the dye pot along with enough water to submerge them. Heat the pot and keep it simmering for an hour before turning off the heat. Soak the leaves in the water for a day before removing them.

Dyeing the fabric
Place the fabric in the dye, add more water if needed and gently simmer for 30 minutes to an hour before leaving the fabric to soak until you're happy with the colour.

Note: because it's so highly scented, the smell of the lavender when it's heating up can become quite overpowering, so it's a good idea to dye in a well ventilated space with a few extra windows open.

woad leaves

A famous plant dye and source of natural indigo, woad leaves have been used to produced a beautiful blue for several thousand years

Latin name: *Isatis tinctoria* **Common name:** Woad
Type: Biannual

Part of the cabbage family, woad grows up to a metre tall, has blueish-green leaves and produces small yellow flowers in its second year. The plant has a very long tap root and this, combined with the fact that it readily self seeds, means that it's often considered to be a pest. Despite searching, I've yet to come across many patches of woad growing in the wild, so I recommend that you grow it from seed in your garden.

Woad seeds are easy to get hold of online and these can be sown outside once the soil has warmed up in the spring. Sew them under a little shelter, in full sun or partial shade, in well-drained soil. Alternatively, the seeds can be sown in seed trays, before planting out once all the risk of frost has passed. In order to prevent the plant from self-seeding all round your garden, make sure you cut back the flowers once they appear in the second year. Leave a few flowers on the plant to produce seeds, which can be saved for sewing the following year.

The leaves will be ready to harvest from July through to the end of September, and should be used as soon after harvesting as possible. If you're unable to use the leaves immediately, then they can be stored in a plastic bag in a cool place to help prevent them from drying out, but the colour results might not be as vibrant as using fresh leaves. Cut the newer leaves from the plant, avoiding any older leaves, because these will no longer contain the chemical in them that makes the blue dye.

Wood leaf dye recipe

Colour: Blue

You will need: 500g freshly harvested wood leaves; ice, soda ash*; pH strips; hand whisk; sodium dithionite**; sugar thermometer.

This is the most technical dye recipe in this book. Although I like to keep plant dyeing as simple as possible, the precise timings and temperatures in this recipe are worth sticking to for the brilliant blue result, which is a rare colour to achieve with plant dyes.

*Soda ash is easy to get hold of online. It's commonly sold as a dye fixer and is also known as sodium carbonate. Soda ash is classed as being non-toxic, but it can cause mild irritation, so wear protective clothing when handling it.

**Another non-toxic powder that requires protective clothing to be worn. Often confused with thiourea dioxide.

Making the dye

1. Fill your dye pot with 5ltr water and heat it to 90C, making sure it doesn't boil (use a sugar thermometer to check the temperature). Once it has reached 90C, turn off the heat, place the wood leaves in the dye pot, and put the lid on to keep in the heat.

2. Set a timer so that the leaves are soaking in the pot for 20 minutes and, in the meantime, fill up the sink with cold water and ice. Once the 20 minutes have passed, remove the lid and place the dye pot into the iced water so that it quickly cools down to 50C. The aim is for the pot to cool down in less than 10 minutes, so you may have to refresh the iced water to encourage it to cool more quickly.

3. Once the pot has reached 50C, strain the dye and place it back into the pot. Be careful and wear gloves for this as the dye will still be hot. At this stage, the dye will look brown, but this is normal as wood requires a few extra steps in order for it to turn blue.

4. Dissolve 2tsp soda ash in a little bit of hot water and add it to the dye pot. Use a pH strip to check that the alkalinity of the liquid is reading at 9 or above and add a little bit more soda ash if it isn't.

5. Add oxygen to the liquid by whisking it until a froth appears. This should take about 10 minutes, during which time the froth normally goes from blue to green.

6. After the oxygen has been added to the dye, it needs to be reduced, which means that the oxygen now needs to be taken back out again. This will enable the blue dye to permanently stick to fabric. The easiest way to do this is to add 2tsp of sodium dithionite

to the dye and replace the lid. Don't stir the dye at this point as this will incorporate more air and oxygen.

7. For the next 30 minutes to an hour the dye needs to be kept between 40-50C, so check the temperature regularly, and put it on a low simmer if it begins to dip too low. After 30 minutes to an hour the dye will turn a translucent greenish yellow colour which means that it's ready.

Dyeing the fabric

1. Once the temperature of the dye has reached 40-50C, place the fabric into the dye. No extra water should be added at this stage, as it will add more oxygen to the dye. Make sure that the fabric is fully submerged, taking care not to agitate the liquid too much because this will add oxygen.

2. Leave the fabric in the dye for 10 minutes before gently lifting it out and squeezing the excess liquid into a bucket.

3. When the fabric is exposed to the air it will turn from a yellow-green colour to blue after 10-15 minutes. Once the blue has developed, the fabric can be dipped into the dye for a second time if you require a darker shade.

4. Once all the fabric has been dyed, place a scrap of fabric into the dye pot and leave it overnight. This will absorb all of the remaining dye and allow you to safely dispose of the liquid.

St John's Wort flower dye recipe

Colour: Terracotta/pinky red

You will need: 20 to 30 flowers.

Making the dye
Put the flowers in a dye pot with enough water to cover them, and gently simmer for 10 minutes. Turn the heat off and leave the flowers soaking in the water for 1-2 days to let the colour develop.

Dyeing the fabric
Place the fabric in the dye and heat it on a gentle simmer for 10 minutes before turning off the heat. You may have to do this several times over the course of a few days for the fabric to absorb enough of the colour.

st john's wort flowers

St John's wort is named so because of the tradition of it flowering on St John's Day. It's frequently used in traditional medicine, and the flowers produce a wonderful terracotta pinky-red dye

Latin name: *Hypericum* **Common name:** St John's wort
Type: Evergreen or deciduous shrub

There are many varieties of St John's wort, but they all have attractive bright yellow flowers in the summer, followed by red or orange berries in the autumn or winter.

St John's wort is happiest in either full sun or part shade, in all (except very damp) soils. It's easy to look after, only requiring a prune in the early spring to encourage more flowers. It will flower on the current season's growth, so cut back the previous year's stems to one or two buds from the framework of the plant. It's often seen as part of a low-maintenance display in public areas, or growing as an informal hedge in gardens. Be warned, however, it will happily self-seed everywhere – most years I even have it growing out of my lawn!

The bright yellow flowers make a wonderful red dye. They can be picked off as they bloom, and stored in the freezer until enough have been collected to use for dye. If it's a large plant, you might even be able to harvest enough flowers in one go.

St John's wort is easily available to buy as a plant, but if you want to grow it from seed bear in mind that the germination rate can be slow and erratic even when the conditions are ideal (which is surprising, considering the rate at which it can self-seed around the garden). It's worth asking a friend or neighbour if they have any St John's wort growing in their garden, as they're likely to have some self-seeded plants that you may be able to dig up and plant in your own garden.

summer project: embroidered picnic blanket

The great thing about this fabulous picnic blanket is that, because it's made from linen, it's really lightweight, which makes it ideal for rolling up and quickly squeezing into your bag for a last-minute jaunt. It can also double up as tablecloth or be used as a throw on the sofa

Things you will need:

- 150cm x 150cm piece of medium-weight linen, dyed with goldenrod flowers and cut into a circle for the main part of the blanket. It's best to use a fabric with a relatively close weave as this will be easier to embroider.

- 5 metre piece of plain, neutral-coloured cotton fringing. I used a 5cm width in this project.

- 1 skein of undyed cotton embroidery floss*, dyed with lavender leaves.

- 1 skein of undyed cotton embroidery floss, dyed with buddleja flowers.

- 1 skein of undyed cotton embroidery floss, dyed with woad leaves.

- 1 skein of undyed cotton embroidery floss, dyed with St John's wort flowers.

- 1 skein of undyed cotton embroidery floss, left undyed.

- Embroidery needles.

- Unbleached cotton thread.

- Heat transfer pen.

- Tracing paper.

- Embroidery hoop.

The hand-stitched embroidery is a slow process and takes time, so it's the perfect project to take with you on days out or during the longer summer evenings. The cotton embroidery thread dyes really well, and produces lovely bright colours

 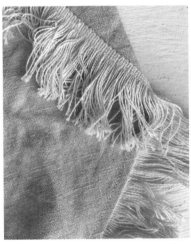

1. Begin by attaching the fringing to the edge of the fabric. Place the fringe on the front of the blanket, edge to edge. Make sure the nicer looking side of the fringing (if there is any difference) is facing upwards. Stitch along the point where the woven edge of the fringing joins the fabric. Once you've sewn around the whole perimeter of the blanket and you're back where you started sewing, overlap the ends of the fringing over by a few centimetres before stitching the end down and cutting off the excess. This will conceal the join of the two ends of fringing.

2. Turn under the fringing and sew the edge down, keeping the stitches close to the edge of the fringing and concealing the rough edge of the picnic blanket fabric. Remember that this stitch will show through on the other side of the blanket, so keep the stitching as neat as possible.

3. The next stage is to transfer the embroidery design onto the fabric. Size up the embroidery design by 50% before placing a piece of tracing paper over it and using a heat transfer pen to trace the design onto the paper. Place the piece of paper onto the fabric and press it with a hot iron for a few seconds to transfer the design. Don't use steam as this will cause the pen to smudge. Using the embroidery threads, stitch the floral design onto the fabric.

Embroidery floss typically comes in skeins that are 8m long with 6 individual strands wound together.

If yours are different, then adjust the amount accordingly. It's always better to dye a little more than you need and have some left over, rather than to run out mid-way through a project and have to try to repeat the same colour in a new dye batch.

chapter nine: autumn

Autumn brings a shift in the atmosphere. Colours become deeper, flowers are slowly replaced by berries, and nuts ripen and fall. It can be easy to think that the autumn and winter months provide less dye material, but there's plenty to find throughout the cooler months

dahlia flowers

It's said that there's a dahlia to suit every taste. With colours ranging from highlighter pen yellow through blush pinks to the deepest of reds, these flamboyant flowers produce yellow, orange and russet brown dye

Latin name: *Dahlia* **Common name:** Dahlia

Type: Tuberous-rooted perennial

Dahlia flowers can range from petite pom-poms, to the size of a dinner plate. They have green (sometimes purple) leaves and the larger varieties tend to have thick, hollow stems that need to be staked to keep the heavy blooms from falling over. During the summer months, the plants should be given a liquid tomato feed (or similar) every fortnight or so to encourage lots of flowers. Frequently grown as part of a bedding display or in a herbaceous border, dahlias like full sun and well-drained soil. Dahlias are tender perennials, but can be overwintered easily. In autumn, carefully dig up the tubers and store them somewhere cool and dry before planting out again when the weather warms up.

Harvest dahlia flowers regularly throughout the growing season to encourage more blooms. The large multi-petalled flowers are the ideal hiding place for insects, so inspect them carefully before putting them in the dye pot. The colour of the flowers doesn't represent the colour of the dye that's produced, which range from yellows, oranges and reds.

Dahlia flower dye recipe

Colour: Yellow/orange/rich reddish browns.

You will need: 8 dahlia flowers. To achieve this colour I used a variety called 'black fox', which make a lovely rich brown shade.

Making the dye
Put the flowers in the dye pot with enough water to just cover them. Heat to a very gentle simmer for a few minutes before turning off the heat and keeping the lid off so the water cools down quickly. They'll begin to release their colour almost immediately (especially if using one of the varieties with deep red colours flowers). After 30 minutes or so, all of the colour will have been extracted and the dye can be strained.

Dyeing the fabric
Place the fabric in the dye and heat it until it reaches a very gentle simmer before turning off the heat and leaving the fabric to soak overnight.

73

Walnut shell dye recipe

Colour: Light brown/dark brown/near-black

You will need: Shells from 20 to 25 walnuts.

Making the dye
Put the brown shells in the dye pot with enough water to cover them and simmer for a couple of hours. It takes several days of simmering and soaking the shells for them to release enough colour to make a dye, so over 2-3 days bring them to a simmer and then turn off the heat several times.

Dyeing the fabric
Place the fabric in the dye and add enough water so that it's fully submerged. Bring the dye to a simmer and leave it for 30 minutes to an hour before turning off the heat. Leave the fabric soaking in the dye for several days. You may have to bring the dye to a simmer several more times to help the dyeing process.

walnut shells

Commonly seen growing around the UK, the walnut tree – with its beautiful, dense canopy – provides both edible nuts and timber. Walnut shells produce a range of warm, autumnal brown dyes

Latin name: *Juglans regia* **Common name:** Common walnut
Type: Large deciduous tree

Walnut trees have large leaves and small catkins that are followed by edible nuts. The trees grow large and take several years to produce nuts, so rather than growing one in your garden, it's easiest to forage for walnut shells from trees in the wild. The trees prefer soil that's not too sandy or clayey and are often found growing in large gardens and parks. During the autumn months there will be plenty of fallen nuts to collect.

The edible walnuts grow inside a hard shell, which is in a protective green hull, and it's the hard shells and green hulls that are used to make a dye. Green hulls that are collected from the common walnut trees (*Juglans regia*) create a dark brown dye; those collected from black walnut tree (*Juglans nigra*) make an almost-black dye. The hard shells from both trees make a light brown colour.

After collecting the green hulls, separate them from the nuts inside and use them immediately by soaking them in water for several days in the same method as for the walnut shells (see opposite). You need to work fast: if the green hulls are stored they'll begin to quickly rot and leech a dark brown dye that stains everything it touches.

It's also possible to obtain a dye from the walnut wood. If you know any carpenters or craftspeople that work with walnut, it's worth asking them to save you some wood shavings because they make a delicate light brown colour.

WALNUT

elderberries

The elderberry tree is one of my favourite plants. I like to keep a note of where I see it growing so that I can go back for harvests in the spring and autumn. The berries produce muted purple and grey dye

Latin name: *Sambucus* **Common name:** Elderberry/elderflower

Type: Herbaceous perennial or small tree

The elderberry plant has small frothy looking creamy/yellow flowers in the late spring followed by deep red and purple berries in the autumn. Elderberry grows well in most conditions, as long as it gets a bit of sunshine. You can often see it in hedgerows, but it also makes a fantastic low-maintenance garden plant. Simply prune it in late winter or early spring to remove any dead or damaged growth.

When harvesting elderberries for dye, use scissors to cut off a whole sprig rather than individual berries. This avoids getting too messy, and ensures plenty of berries are left on the plant for birds to eat.

Of course, elderberry plants also produce flowers, which are often harvested and turned into delicious cordials earlier on in the year. Bear in mind that if you're harvesting the flowers as well as the berries, you'll need to leave plenty of flowers on the plant to allow them to mature into the berries.

Elderberry dye recipe

Colour: Purple and grey

You will need: 10 to 15 sprigs of elderberries.

Making the dye
Put the berries in the dye pot, making sure that there's enough water so they're fully submerged. Bring them to a gentle simmer, turn off the heat immediately and leave them to soak for a few hours until the dye has cooled.

Dyeing the fabric
Place the fabric in the dye, turn on the heat and let it simmer gently for 30 minutes before leaving the fabric to soak for one to two days.

It's almost impossible to achieve a long lasting colour from berries of any sort, and quite often a dramatic colour change occurs after they've been washed because the colour adjusts according to the pH of the water and soap used. Additionally, I'd only recommend using elderberry-dyed fabric for items that don't need frequent washing as the colour is prone to fading.

Dyers chamomile flower dye recipe

Colour: Yellow

You will need: approximately 50 flowers.

Making the dye
Put the flowers in the dye pot with enough water to just cover them. Heat to a very gentle simmer for a few minutes before switching off the heat and removing the lid so the water begins to cool down quickly. Leave them in the water overnight to extract all the colour.

Dyeing the fabric
Place the fabric in the dye and top it up with water, if needed. Heat the dye until it reaches a very gentle simmer before turning off the heat and leaving the fabric to soak in the dye overnight.

dyers chamomile flowers

Dyers chamomile is a cheerful-looking plant to have in the garden, but it's often confused with other types of chamomile that don't produce a dye. The daisy-like flowers produce a warm yellow dye

Latin name: *Anthemis tinctoria* **Common name:** Dyers chamomile

Type: Herbaceous perennial. Replace every two years as it tends to get spindly

All chamomile plants have fine green leaves and daisy-like flowers. Dyers chamomile has brilliant yellow flower heads and aromatic foliage. It's unlikely that you'll find enough dyers chamomile in the wild to be able to make dye, so it's best to grow it in your garden. Dyers chamomile plants are easy to get hold of, or you can grow it from seed in spring. Start them off in seed trays in a greenhouse (or sunny windowsill) and once all risk of frost has passed, scatter them directly onto the flowerbed where you want them to grow.

It likes to be grown in well-drained soil, will thrive in full sun and produces more flowers if it's deadheaded. It flowers from mid-summer right the way through to the early autumn. At the end of the growing season, the tiny seeds can be saved for sowing next year, but they're so small that it's best to cut off the whole dried flower head and store it in a paper bag.

Quite a lot of flowers are needed to make a decent amount of dye, but they can be picked as they flower and stored in the freezer until you've collected enough.

Achillea flower dye recipe

Colour: Greenish yellow

You will need: 10 to 15 flower heads.

Making the dye
Put the flowers in a dye pot with enough water to cover them and let them simmer gently for 10 minutes, before turning off the heat and leaving them to soak for 1-2 days to let the colour develop.

Dyeing the fabric
Place the fabric in the dye with some extra water if it's needed and bring it to a gentle simmer for around 30 minutes. Turn off the heat and leave the fabric to soak in the dye for 1-2 days.

yarrow flowers

A useful medicinal herb, yarrow is a lovely little plant that seems to grow almost anywhere, and its flat white flower heads are easily spotted when out on autumn walks. It produces a delicate greenish yellow dye

Latin name: *Achillea millefolium* **Common name:** Yarrow
Type: Deciduous perennial

The yarrow that's most commonly found growing in grass and in the wild is Achillea millefolium and has clusters of small, white flowers. There are many varieties cultivated for our gardens, which have a range of different coloured flowers, which all produce the same yellow-green dye.

Yarrow plants like full sun, but they'll grow in nearly any soil and will happily self-seed. To harvest for dyeing, simply cut off the whole flower heads, leaving the foliage to allow more flowers to grow. Towards the end of the season, leave some of the flowers on the plant so that it can produce seeds and spread to other parts of the garden. If you spot a self-seeded yarrow plant in a patio or somewhere where is isn't wanted, it can be lifted out gently and planted in a pot.

autumn project: hot water bottle cosy

A hot water bottle is a great thing to have on hand as the nights draw in and start to get cooler. It can even be the perfect accompaniment on an autumn walk tucked inside your coat, and this cover makes it extra warm and toasty!

Things you will need:

- 140cm x 100cm piece of medium-weight cotton calico for the lining, left undyed.

- 40cm x 100cm piece of medium-weight cotton calico for the outside of the cosy, dyed with elderberries.

- 40cm x 100cm piece of wadding for the insulation layer. I used a wool wadding for this project.

- Wool to make the pom-poms. I used one 100g ball of merino wool, which makes lovely soft pom-poms. Split the ball into four parts and dye the wool with the dahlia flowers, walnut shells, yarrow flowers and chamomile flowers.

- Cardboard from an old cereal box for making the pom-poms.

- Unbleached cotton thread.

This brilliant little project needs hardly any fabric, and it's quick to make. The wool pom-poms in tonal shades add a quirky finishing touch

1. To begin, sandwich each piece of wadding between the lining and outer pieces and pin them together.

2. Sew diagonal stitches 3cm apart to secure the fabric layers together. You can use a piece of masking tape to help you stitch them in a straight line.

3. Next, stitch diagonal lines at a 45-degree angle to the first row of stitches, making a grid pattern on the fabric. Make sure that all the lines are sewn in the same direction to avoid the fabric from bubbling up and looking messy. The fabric will naturally shift sightly as you sew, but this doesn't matter too much because the fabric is slightly larger than the finished hot water bottle cosy size.

4. Scale up the pattern pieces and copy them onto the right side of the fabric before cutting them out. Using a zig-zag stitch, sew around the edges of all of the pattern pieces to stop them fraying.

5. Fold over the 'fold line' (shown on the pattern) towards the inside of the cosy. Press and then hand stitch in place. Fold them over by 1cm and hand stitch them in place using a slip stitch. Make sure the stitches don't show on the outside of the hot water bottle cosy.

6. Overlap the two back pieces, lining up the notches on the pattern, making sure that the back-bottom piece is underneath the back-top piece. Stitch them together, sewing very close to the edge so that the stitches won't be visible later.

7. Place the front and back pieces together with the right sides together and line up the notches. Stitch them together using a 1cm seam allowance. Snip off the corners, being careful not to cut into the stitching and then turn the hot water bottle cosy the right way out.

8. To make the pom-poms, cut out two 7cm diameter cardboard circles – an old cereal packet will do. Cut a slit in the circles and cut out a central circle that has a 3cm diameter. You should be left with what looks like a ring doughnut with a slice cut out of it. Place the doughnuts together.

9. Loop the end of a piece of wool round the doughnuts and begin to wind the wool around them. Continue winding the wool until several layers have built up. Try to keep the wool distributed evenly around the cardboard doughnut as this create a neater pom-pom.

10. Once the piece of cardboard is completly covered, cut the end of the wool so that it leaves a few centimetres spare.

11. Holding onto the wool so that it doesn't fall out of the hole, insert your scissors between the two doughnut layers and cut the wool.

12. Cut another piece of wool approximately 20cm long, and push it between the two cardboard doughnuts and tie it in a knot. Wrap it round and tie it in a knot several times to make sure that the pom-pom is really secure.

13. Remove the cardboard template and carefully trim the pom-pom to neaten up the edges and give it a fuller look.

14. Make four pom-poms in total, each from a different colour of wool, and then stitch them onto the front of the hot water bottle cosy.

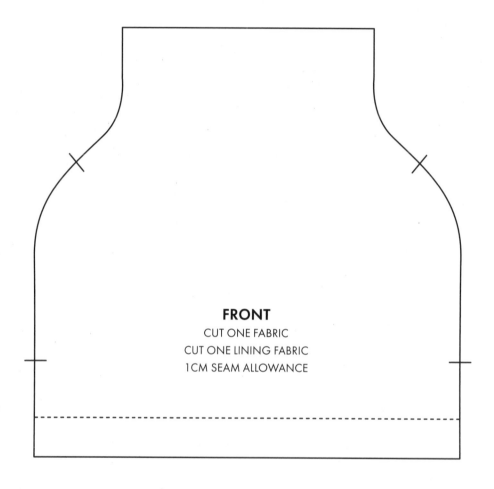

FRONT
CUT ONE FABRIC
CUT ONE LINING FABRIC
1CM SEAM ALLOWANCE

Before tracing and cutting out the pattern, enlarge it by 50% and print it out.
This will make a cover big enough to fit a standard 2ltr (28cm x 20cm) hot water bottle.

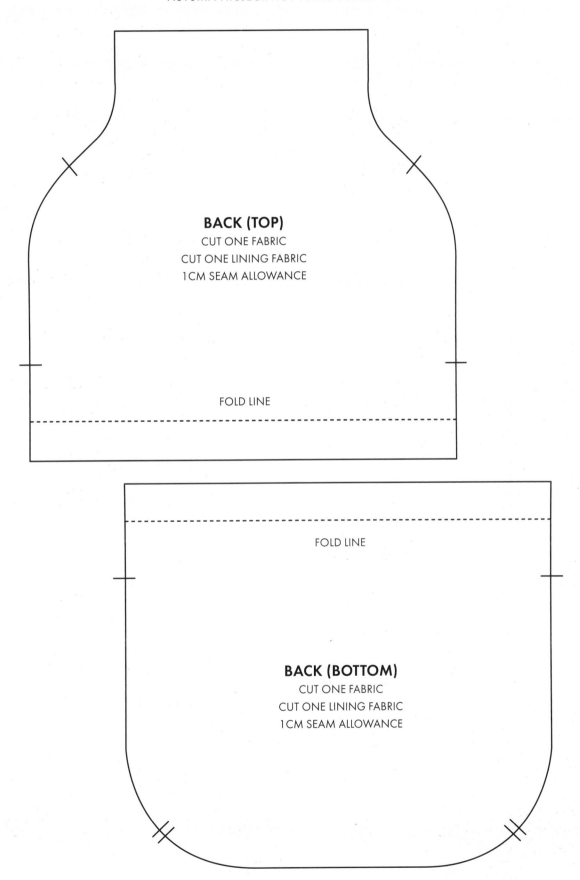

BACK (TOP)
CUT ONE FABRIC
CUT ONE LINING FABRIC
1CM SEAM ALLOWANCE

FOLD LINE

FOLD LINE

BACK (BOTTOM)
CUT ONE FABRIC
CUT ONE LINING FABRIC
1CM SEAM ALLOWANCE

chapter ten: winter

Evergreen plants can provide lots of sources of dye during the winter months. But look a little deeper and you can find other ways to create a plant dye: alder cones and bark that has blown off trees in a storm, nuts and berries, and even the odd winter flower to keep the dye pot brimming throughout the winter

rosemary leaves

Each winter, I cut lots of rosemary to decorate the house and to make dye. Around Christmas time, it gives a lovely and natural festive scent. The leaves produce a grey (and sometimes purple) dye

Latin name: *Rosmarinus* **Common name**: Rosemary

Type: Evergreen shrub

Rosemary has narrow, highly scented leaves and small blue flowers that appear from spring through to the autumn. It likes well drained soil in full sun, and is easy to maintain once it's established in the garden. Like lavender, rosemary tends to grow really well from cuttings and it's a great way to cheaply increase the number of plants (see Lavender leaves, on page 61, for guidance on how to take cuttings). It's often used as an informal hedge or boundary in public areas, such as parks.

Older rosemary leaves tend to make stronger colours than the fresh growth in spring, so it's better to wait until the winter to harvest the plant. Try not to harvest too much of the plant at once, and harvest from all over the whole plant, rather than concentrating on one area. If it's pruned into a formal shape, bear this in mind when harvesting from the plant.

Typically, rosemary produces a gorgeous grey dye that seems to change colour, depending on which other plant colours it's matched with. Occasionally, it's possible to produce a purple dye from rosemary, but this is entirely dependant on the variety and age of the leaves that are being used, so it's well worth experimenting with lots of different rosemary cuttings to see which colours they produce. The very dark grey colour here was created by dyeing fabric with rosemary leaves and then dipping it in an iron water solution (see page 37).

Rosemary leaf dye recipe

Colour: Grey, but sometimes purple

You will need: 4 very generous handfuls of rosemary leaves that have been separated from the stems.

Making the dye
Put the rosemary leaves in the dye pot along with enough water to submerge them. Heat the pot and keep it simmering for an hour before turning off the heat. Soak the leaves in the water for a day before removing them.

Dyeing the fabric
Place the fabric in the dye, add more water if needed and simmer gently for 30 minutes to an hour before leaving the fabric to soak until you're happy with the colour.

Note: Similar to lavender, rosemary leaves are highly scented. It's advisable to extract this dye in a well-ventilated area as the scent intensifies and becomes quite overpowering as it's heated up in the dye pot.

Ivy leaf dye recipe

Colour: Greenish grey

You will need: half a bucket full of ivy leaves (the occasional bit of stem is fine).

Making the dye
Put the ivy the dye pot with enough water to cover it. I find that ivy produces better, darker shades if it's allowed to boil for 10 minutes, and then bought down to a simmer. Once it has simmered for 30 minutes, turn off the heat and allow the leaves to soak in the water overnight.

Dyeing the fabric
Place the fabric in the dye, adding a little extra water, if needed, and heat it to a simmer for an hour before turning off the heat, letting the dye cool before the fabric is removed.

ivy leaves

Ivy is seen as both a pest in our gardens and also as a plant that can give a feeling of age and a sense of old fashioned whimsy to places where it grows. The leaves produce a greenish grey dye

Latin name: *Hedra helix* **Common name:** Common ivy
Type: Evergreen climber

Common ivy is happy growing pretty much anywhere, its dark green glossy leaves quickly cover an area of ground, fence or tree trunk, which means it can easily be picked up on walks through towns and countryside. It has small yellow flowers in the autumn, followed by dark green or purple berries in the winter.

Ivy has roots that cling to the surface that it grows on. If you're harvesting it from walls, it's better to cut it rather than pull it out if you want to avoid damaging mortar. Both the leaves and stems can be collected to make dye, but try to avoid harvesting the flowers or berries: they don't make the dye colour seen here, and provide a valuable source of food for insects and birds during the winter months, when food is scarce.

Eucalyptus leaf dye recipe

Colour: Orange

You will need: 5-6 handfuls of eucalyptus leaves (they can be kept on the stems).

Making the dye
Put the leaves in the dye pot, along with enough water to submerge them. Heat the pot and keep it simmering for one hour before turning off the heat. Leave the leaves soaking in the water for 2-3 days before removing them, bringing them to a simmer for 10 minutes on several occasions during this time.

Dyeing the fabric
Place the fabric in the dye and add extra water to make sure it's fully submerged. Heat the dye and leave it simmering for an hour, before turning off the heat. Leave the fabric to soak in the dye overnight.

eucalyptus leaves

Eucalyptus is said to improve respiratory health as well as reducing anxiety and stress. When the leaves are heated in the dye pot, they release a beautiful aroma. The leaves produce a rusty-orange dye

Latin name: *Eucalyptus* **Common name:** Eucalyptus
Type: Fast-growing evergreen tree

There are several varieties of eucalyptus commonly grown in the UK, many of which tend to have rounded grey-green leaves that are highly scented, plus clusters of yellow, white or red flowers in the spring. Along with the leaves, flaking and peeling bark can be collected for dyeing (the bark produces a different dye colour to the leaves).

Once planted, eucalyptus is fairly low maintenance, so you'll find it in parks, public areas and domestic gardens. When harvesting leaves from the tree, whole sections of small branches can be cut with secateurs. When collecting bark, wait until it has fallen to the ground – never pull it away from the trunk as this can damage the tree and risk introducing infection.

Eucalyptus is often used in bunches of cut flowers, particularly at Christmas time, so these can be saved for dyeing. It dries very well, and can be stored easily until you've collected enough for the dye pot.

Alder cone dye recipe

Colour: Greenish light brown

You will need: Approximately 100 alder cones.

Making the dye
Put the alder cones in the dye pot with just enough water to cover them, and bring to a simmer for 30 minutes. Leave them to soak for 1-2 days.

Dyeing the fabric
Place the fabric in the dye and add some extra water until it's fully submerged. Heat the dye and leave it to simmer for an hour, before turning off the heat. Remove the fabric once the dye has cooled.

alder cones

Alder trees are steeped in folklore and history, and it's said that putting alder leaves in your shoes on a long walk will stop your feet from getting too tired. The cones produce a greenish-toned light brown dye

Latin name: *Alnus glutinosa* **Common name:** Alder

Type: Large deciduous tree

Growing up to 25 metres tall, the alder tree belongs to the birch family, and has shiny, rounded bright green leaves. Both the male and female trees produce catkins (male catkins are long and yellow), but only female oval-shaped green catkins become woody alder cones when pollinated.

Alder cones normally stay on the tree all year round, but winter is the ideal time to harvest them because the lack of leaves on the tree makes them easier to spot. You may find that after periods of high wind the ground below the tree is littered with fallen cones, which can be collected for dyeing.

Alder trees are able to thrive in poor wet conditions, and are often found near rivers and ponds.

Dyer alkanet root dye recipe

Colour: Purple

You will need: an equal weight of dried alkanet roots to your fabric.

Making the dye
Soak the alkanet roots in water for around two weeks until the water turns a brownish purple. During this time, the water should be simmered several times for 30 minutes at a time, to encourage the roots to release their colour.

Dyeing the fabric
Place the fabric into the dye and add a little extra water, if needed, to ensure the fabric is fully submerged. Heat the dye to a simmer for an hour before turning off the heat and leaving the fabric to soak for several days. This dye smells particularly unpleasant, so do this in a well ventilated area.

dyers alkanet roots

Perhaps the most unusual plant in this book, alkanet has historically been used to colour a variety of items and, in some countries, is still used in food and drink. The root produces a soft purple dye

Latin name: *Alkanna tinctoria* **Common name:** Dyers alkanet
Type: Herbaceous perennial

Dyers alkanet has small, sky-blue flowers and grey leaves. It looks similar to green alkanet (*Entaglottis sempervirens*), which doesn't work as a dye, but it's easy to spot the difference because green alkanet has greener foliage and flowers that are a more purple-blue colour.

Since they're rarely spotted in the wild, it's best to grow dyers alkanet from seed in your garden. The seeds are fairly difficult to buy, and tend to have a low germination rate, but once these little plants are growing in your garden you can let them self-seed for future harvests. They grow best in sandy soil in full sun and will produce a rosette of leaves in their first year, followed by sky-blue flowers in their second year. As it's the roots that are harvested for dyeing, it's best to collect these after the second year, once the plant has flowered and set seed. This means you can put some seeds aside, in case the plant is damaged accidentally when harvesting the roots.

During the late winter, dig up the alkanet plants and carefully trim off about 50 per cent of the roots, before planting them back in the ground. Once harvested, the roots should be washed thoroughly to remove all the soil, and then left to dry. When dried, they'll store for several years, which is ideal if you can only harvest a small amount of alkanet roots at a time.

Fabric dyed with alkanet root tends to fade when washed too much or left in direct sunlight for a prolonged period of time, so bear this in mind when deciding what you're going to dye.

winter project: patchwork quilt

This patchwork project can be gradually put together over the colder winter months, and you can either follow this design or make up your own, sewing pieces together as they're dyed

Things you will need to make a 150cm x 140cm quilt:

- 150cm x 150cm piece of medium-weight cotton or linen (I used cotton) for the back of the quilt, dyed with eucalyptus leaves.

- 60cm x 220cm piece of medium-weight cotton or linen (I used linen) for the front of the quilt, dyed with alder cones.

- 60cm x 220cm piece of medium-weight cotton or linen (I used linen) for the front of the quilt, dyed with rosemary leaves and then dipped in iron water.

- 60cm x 220cm piece of medium-weight cotton or linen (I used linen) for the front of the quilt, dyed with ivy leaves.

- 60cm x 220cm piece of medium-weight cotton or linen (I used linen) for the front of the quilt, dyed with eucalyptus leaves.

- 60cm x 220cm piece of medium-weight cotton or linen (I used linen) for the front of the quilt, dyed with alkanet roots.

- A 60cm x 250cm piece of medium-weight cotton or linen (I used linen) for the front of the quilt, left undyed.

- 6.5m piece of cotton bias binding, left undyed.

- 150cm x 150cm piece of wadding. For this project I used a wool wadding, as it makes a cosy and warm quilt for the winter. Polyester provides thickness without the weight of wool. It's best to use a cotton wadding if you're machine quilting, as hand stitching tends to be trickier with cotton wadding as the cotton tends to 'drag' on the needle. There are also waddings available that are blends of different fibres. If needed, narrower pieces of wadding can be joined together by butting them up to each other and securing them with a zig-zag stitch on a sewing machine.

- Unbleached cotton thread.

- Unbleached cotton hand quilting thread (for hand quilting only).

- Safety pins.

- A rotary cutter and cutting mat or tailor's chalk/ vanishing fabric pen and scissors (depending on how you'd like to cut out your patchwork fabric).

1. Cut out the following number of 15cm x 15cm fabric squares:
36 dyed with eucalyptus leaves
36 dyed with rosemary leaves
36 dyed with alkanet roots
36 dyed with ivy leaves
52 dyed with alder cones
44 undyed

2. Cut each of the squares in half to create two triangles. Referring to the quilt on page 100, put the triangles in order in ten different piles, numbered 1 to 10, left to right. You should end up with ten different piles, made up of 24 triangles that are stacked in the order that they join together to form the quilt.

3. Referring again to the quilt on page 100, stitch the triangles together along the diagonal edge using a 1cm seam allowance* to form a square, keeping them in order and putting them back in their ten piles as they're sewn.

*Note: it's important to stay as accurate to this seam allowance as possible, so that the lines of the quilt match up and the finished quilt looks neat.

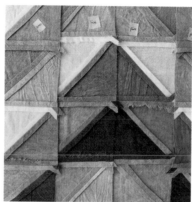

4. Once all of the triangles have been sewn together to form squares, press the seams open with an iron, being careful to keep them in order. Although pressing the seams is rather time consuming, it will help to reduce any bulk at the seams, which will make the following steps easier.

5. Starting from pile number one (the left-hand side of the quilt), stitch the squares together so they form a long row, making sure the square from the top of the pile is at the top of the row. After this is done, do the same for the remaining piles. Once again, press the seams open.

6. Place rows one and two together, double checking which side of row one is the outside-left edge of the quilt. Sew the rows together, making sure the seams match up. Repeat this for the other rows until the front of the quilt is constructed. Press the seams open.

7. Lay the back piece of fabric out onto a large, flat surface and place the wadding on top. Place the top layer of the quilt onto the wadding and make sure there's an even amount of excess fabric around the edges. Use safety pins to hold the three layers of fabric together.

8. Start from the centre of the quilt and stitch outwards, to prevent the fabrics from shifting as they're sewn. Here I've stitched next to the seams to make a feature of the stitches. There need to be enough stitches to hold the layers of the quilt together. You can either hand or machine stitch your quilt layers together.

9. Once the layers have been stitched together, use a sewing machine to stitch around the edge of the quilt, about 0.5cm in from the edge of the top layer, and then trim off the excess fabric. This will keep the very edges of the quilt together and make it easier to sew on the binding.

10. Start sewing the binding from the middle of an edge to give a neat finish. Place the binding onto the front of the quilt, edge to edge. Fold over the first few centimetres of the binding to hide any raw edges.

11. Sew the binding to the front of the quilt about 1cm from the edge. Keep on sewing the binding until you reach 1cm from the corner and then sew a few back stitches to secure it.

12. Remove the quilt from the sewing machine and fold the binding up over itself to create a 45-degree angle at the corner. This will create a mitered corner, giving the quilt a really neat finish.

13. Fold the biding straight down, keeping the top and side level with the top and side edges of the quilt. Sew the binding on the next side of the quilt, using a 1cm seam allowance, making sure to start the new line of stitches at the point where the previous one finished.

14. When you're almost back at the starting point, overlap the ends of the binding by a few centimetres. Trim off any excess binding and finish sewing.

15. To sew the reverse side of the binding, flip the quilt over and hand stitch the binding down, using a slip stitch and easing the mitered corners in place as you sew.

About the author

So, who am I? I'm Alicia Hall, and I first discovered the magic of making dyes from plants when I stumbled across it in a horticulture book. After months of colourful experiments with plants and fabrics, I started my business, Botanical Threads. Discovering that I could make dye from plants was a eureka moment for me. I come from a fashion background and completed a degree in Fashion Design before going on to run several small (very, very small) creative businesses in the evenings and weekends, while I worked a series of boring (very, very boring) day jobs. When I bought my first home, I realised that I had to put in some effort if I wanted to have a nice looking garden. This sparked a passion for plants, and I somehow ended up working as a gardener for the National Trust. For several years my head was full of dahlias and daisies. Then I found out about dyeing with plants and realised that I could combine my two passions: my love of horticulture and my enjoyment of making things with fabric. Now I spend my time working on Botanical Threads from my little home studio and going on weekend walks in the countryside with my husband and son. It's slow going as I make them stop every few minutes so that I can take a photo or collect some plants to create a dye, but they don't complain too much!

Acknowledgements

At the start of 2018, I received an email from Katherine Raderecht asking if I'd like to write this book. I thought it was a hoax and almost deleted the email – thank goodness I didn't! Thank you, Katherine, for reaching out to me and providing me with this opportunity. A big thank you also goes to everyone who has supported Botanical Threads over the past few years – whether you've bought something, taken the time to read my blog or kept up with me on Instagram. Without all of you backing me, this never could have happened.
www.botanicalthreads.co.uk @botanical_threads